TABLE OF CONTENTS

Page

ACRONYMS

AQN	Al-Qaeda Network
ASEAN	Association of South East Asian Nations
JCET	Joint Combined Exchange Training
SOF	Special Operations Forces
TNI	Tentara Nasional Indonesia (Indonesian National Defense Force)
U.S.	United States
WW II	World War II

ILLUSTRATIONS

CHAPTER 1

INTRODUCTION

The Pacific Ocean does not separate the United States from Asia; it connects us. We are connected by our economies, by our cultures, by our shared interests, and our security challenges. We have been accepting additional risk in the Indo-Asia-Pacific region for some time. Our rebalance strategy is in place, and we are making progress. Implementing and sustaining the strategic rebalance will require long-term, sustained commitment and resources.

— Admiral Samuel Locklear,
Testimony before the House Armed Services Committee, 2013

Introduction to the Issue

Following redeployment of combat troops from the Middle East, the recent United States (U.S.) security strategy focused on the Asia-Pacific region in 2012. This strategy is commonly referred to as a "pivot" or "shift." There are many subtle aspects to this strategy and the U.S. Department of Defense (DoD) must analyze how, in a fiscally constrained environment, to effectively allocate its available resources to get the best results. The U.S. must prioritize efforts to build partners and allies in the Asia-Pacific region with a look at the long-term benefits within the respective countries engaged, the effects sought for the region and the appearance presented to the rest of the world.

As the U.S. rebalances its foreign policy toward the Pacific, an improved relationship with Indonesia becomes a high priority. Indonesia is an influential country in many aspects and can be tied to the U.S. National Security Strategy 2010s four enduring national interests: Security, Prosperity, Values and International Order. Security—as a large archipelago used by Muslim extremists to conduct attacks, the U.S.-Indonesia partnership is key to pursuing Al-Qaeda Network (AQN) and affiliates. Prosperity—

1

through the global economy with G-20, the straits of Malacca and influence into the South China Sea. Values—Indonesia is an emerging democracy, an example of a civilian led government in the largest Muslim country in the world. International order-as a founding member of the Association of South East Asian Nations (ASEAN), Indonesia weighs heavily to help influence bi-lateral and coalition interests through the region and world. The U.S. can influence all of these with a well-established relationship with the Indonesian government. With minimal strain on the U.S. military, this can be accomplished through engagement with the Indonesian Special Operations Forces (SOF).

Full U.S. SOF partnership with the Indonesian Kopassus (Army Special Forces Command) can have an impact greater than just building a military to military relationship. Due to the Kopassus importance inside Indonesia, a partnership with U.S. SOF can provide influence to internal and external Indonesian military operations, external regional military operations between other regional countries and internal Indonesian political dynamics. The relationship and engagement with the Kopassus needs to be prioritized, analyzed and executed as part of a synchronized whole of government approach in dealing with Indonesia. This relationship, executed correctly, can have an impact that advances U.S. national interests internally within Indonesia and regionally in Southeast Asia for years.

Another advantage gained through SOF partnership engagement is a positive example of the U.S. successfully dealing with a democratically elected, moderate Muslim government and nation. Additionally, China seeks engagement throughout the region and has already begun a relationship with the Kopassus, the U.S. has an opportunity to take part in a multi-lateral relationship in Southeast Asia through the military. This

2

opportunity can provide not only military to military exposure and relationships between all three countries, but also shows the world that a super-power nation and a rising world power can work together with an influential regional Islamic power to ensure regional security and economic viability.

The U.S. has not engaged the Kopassus for more than 12 years, due to numerous human rights allegations during operations dating back to the 1970s—especially in East Timor. The Indonesian Kopassus have no doubt committed human rights violations in the past, not only by U.S. standards, but also by those of the Western world. The senior leadership of the Indonesian Armed Forces, the Tentara Nasional Indonesia (TNI), has recognized this and for the past 10 plus years implemented training and new standards for their forces. However, there are still members of the Kopassus accused of human rights violations, and additional emerging accusations from both past and present operations impacting the U.S.'s engagement strategy with the Indonesian military.

The Leahy Conditions (amendments or laws as often referred), even after their repeal, still hindered U.S. partnership and engagement with the Kopassus for years. In the majority of mainstream and local media reports there is still a strong rejection to any U.S. contact, plan to train or even the general thought of engagement with the Kopassus. International Human Rights groups demand more prosecution of current and former members involved in human rights violations.

The TNI and the Kopassus made substantial progress in the transparency of their operations and prosecution of guilty members when compared to Indonesia of the past. Much more progress is needed in the realms of executing military operations with regard to human rights and prosecution of abusers. Incremental gains however are a positive

3

development, and should be acknowledged and rewarded. Human rights organizations argue for full prosecution of all accused and advocate for the continued denial of military engagement with the Kopassus as the only solution. Department of Defense and SOF argue that without military engagement the unit cannot be monitored or shown "what right looks like" and therefore progress will either be continually slow or reach a natural plateau. No single solution provides a perfect answer for all organizations.

Currently, the U.S. Mission to Indonesia FY 2013 Mission Strategic and Resource Plan lists goal number six of its ten goals, as "Facilitating Reform of Security Forces." In the details of this goal the Mission seeks to initiate reengagement with the Kopassus. Additionally, in March 2013, Admiral Locklear, the United States Pacific Command (USPACOM) Combatant Commander, testified before the House Armed Services Committee that the U.S. will reestablish security cooperation activities with the Kopassus. The decision to reengage has been made by both the civilian policy makers and the highest level of military leaders.

Therefore this thesis does not seek to answer the question of whether it is proper to engage with the Kopassus or for the U.S. to engage with a military unit accused of human rights violations. Nor does it tackle the reforms necessary to repeal the Leahy Conditions and prove progress in a unit. The author realizes that even with attempts at defining what is or is not acceptable by international human rights organizations, U.S. Congress, Department of State and even the United Nations, there are instances and situations which one could use to prosecute "any" military unit, leader or administration in the world. The definitions of human rights and especially the conduct of them in enforcing a country's laws are as varied as the cultures of the United Nations. While there are exact definitions written to certain aspects of torture, detainment, and interrogation, as the last decade of war has shown the world, even those definitions are subject to interpretation. The world constantly tries to come to consensus on the definitions for human rights. However, as soon as a line is drawn a new situation arises which challenges the latest definition. This is not meant to belittle or disparage human rights rules, but rather to highlight how professional judgment must be used as every situation is different and requires informed insight.

This thesis seeks to inform readers of the situation, and analyze possible impacts of America's long disengagement from the Kopassus. The conclusions will show the advantages of implementation of the military instrument of U.S. national power given the recent decision to reengage. Further opportunities are explored, as engagement with the Kopassus should benefit the U.S. in more than just the recovery of a forgotten relationship. There are many other advantages, which could be had not only for the U.S., but also for Indonesia and the region.

Research Question

Figure 1 depicts a flow diagram giving a visual of the primary and secondary research questions, the research directions and pathway to the author's recommendations.

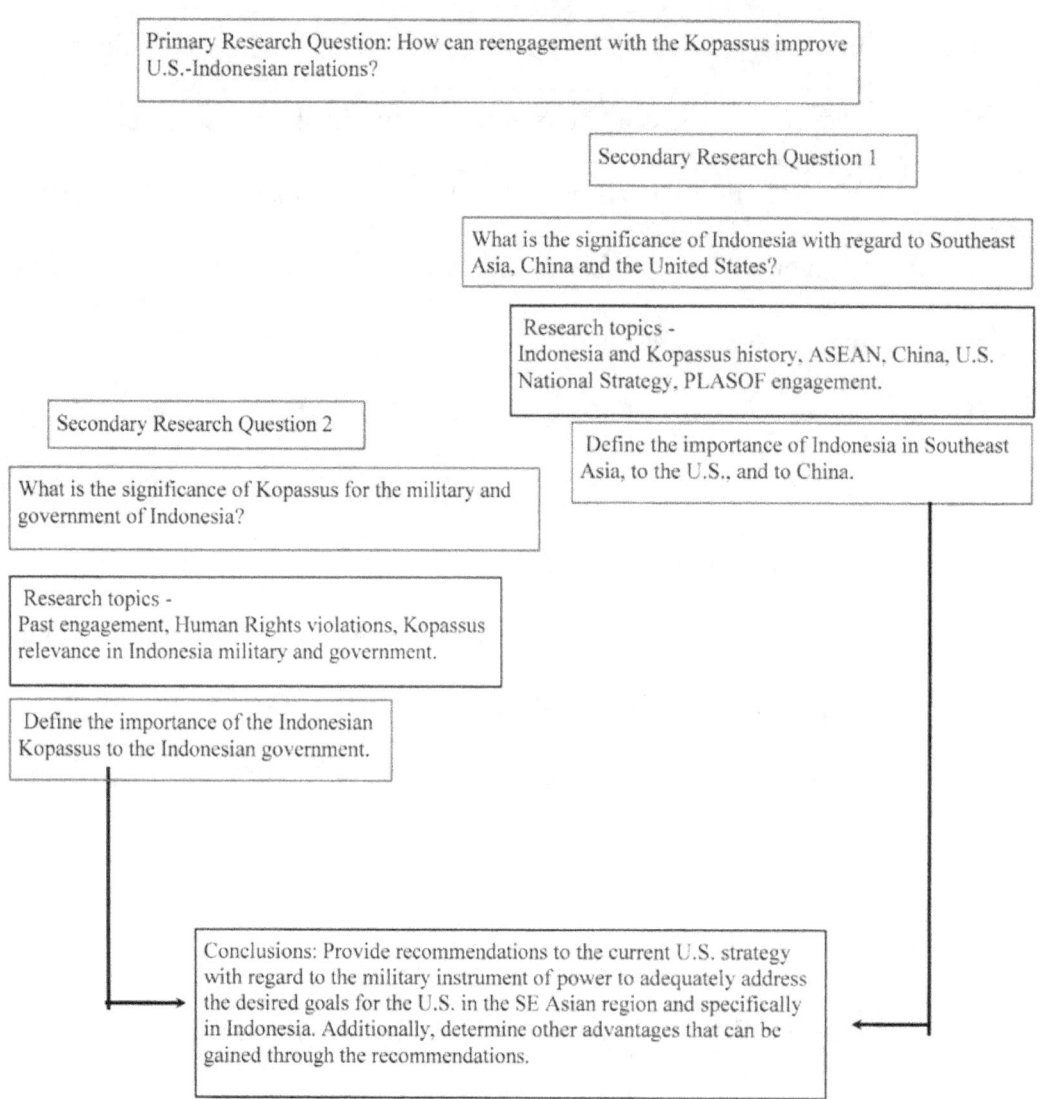

Reengaging the Indonesian Kopassus: Looking at
the Long-term Approach and Getting it Right.

Primary Research Question: How can reengagement with the Kopassus improve
U.S.-Indonesian relations?

Secondary Research Question 1

What is the significance of Indonesia with regard to Southeast
Asia, China and the United States?

Research topics -
Indonesia and Kopassus history, ASEAN, China, U.S.
National Strategy, PLASOF engagement.

Secondary Research Question 2

What is the significance of Kopassus for the military and
government of Indonesia?

Define the importance of Indonesia in Southeast
Asia, to the U.S., and to China.

Research topics -
Past engagement, Human Rights violations, Kopassus
relevance in Indonesia military and government.

Define the importance of the Indonesian
Kopassus to the Indonesian government.

Conclusions: Provide recommendations to the current U.S. strategy
with regard to the military instrument of power to adequately address
the desired goals for the U.S. in the SE Asian region and specifically
in Indonesia. Additionally, determine other advantages that can be
gained through the recommendations.

Figure 1.   Flow Diagram of Research Question

Source: Created by author.

Significance of Study

This thesis explores current U.S. foreign policy position and objectives with regard to Indonesia and more specifically toward the U.S. relationship with the Indonesian Special Forces, the Kopassus. The purpose is to analyze the positive and negative outcomes of limiting the military-to-military interaction with a country's elite forces. While the concept of withholding military aid and interaction for past atrocities briefs well morally, it may actually be hindering forward progress in regional stability, proper application of human rights and securing U.S. national interests.

The U.S. decision to reengage the Kopassus requires strategy execution synchronized with the other elements of U.S. national power to ensure the correct effect is achieved. The value of a strong partnership with Indonesia provides influence for the U.S. with a large democratic Muslim country, an influential founding member of the ASEAN, and a sought after ally for China.

This thesis is designed to provide policy makers, planners and implementers with information to consider regarding the importance and larger strategic effects a relationship with the Kopassus could provide the United States. Because of the timing of the administration's "Pivot to the Pacific" and the decision to announce reengagement specifically with the Kopassus, the relevance of information on the unit's influence is contemporary. The Kopassus are more than just another national military SOF element. The Indonesian military and Kopassus are cornerstone elements to founding the formation of the country, which then established national control over an archipelago nation. The Kopassus quickly responds in efficient and effective manners to current day terrorist threats, which set them up as a part of Indonesian nationalism. The unit provides strong, decisive leaders and the country will use the U.S. engagement with the Kopassus as a metric of U.S. commitment to Indonesia.

Background

Indonesia

Indonesia is the world's fourth most populous country and the largest nation in Southeast Asia. Approximately 86 percent of Indonesians claim Islam as their religion, thereby making Indonesia home to the world's largest Muslim population. Indonesia's form of Islam is consistently considered a moderate form by academics, researchers, authors and international media.[1] This moderate form of Islam allows Indonesia to exercise secular democracy in its government. Thus Indonesia is also the world's third largest democracy.[2] Indonesia is also a member of G-20 and a founding, influential member of ASEAN. The Indonesian government promotes a stance of non-alignment, where it prefers to have all friends and no enemies making gains in any partnership or commitment to any one country difficult.[3]

---

[1]Bruce Vaughn, *Indonesia: Domestic Politics, Strategic Dynamics, and American Interests* (Washington, DC: Congressional Research Service, January 31, 2011), 1.

[2]Department of State, *Mission Strategic and Resource Plan FY 2013*, 1.

[3]Ibid.

Indonesia is a relatively young democracy, gaining independence in the mid-20th century. While it has claimed democracy since its independence after World War II (WW II), historians and authors argue it was more of a military autocracy under Indonesia's first President, Sukarno (alternate Dutch spelling *Soekarno*—known by one name in Indonesia). Sukarno instituted "Guided Democracy," to ensure a peaceful establishment without resistance to the new independent country of Indonesia. Using the guise of Guided Democracy, Sukarno took complete control of media, parliament and the military, instituting his own loyalists as leaders throughout Indonesia.[4] Essentially for the first 20 years of Indonesia's independence, it was actually a semi-socialist state.

---

[4]M. C. Ricklefs, *A History of Modern Indonesia Since C. 1300* (Stanford, CA: Stanford University Press, 1993), 257-283.

The Indonesian government continues to make strides in separating civilian leadership from military control, although more work needs to be done. Indonesians generally support secular, civilian led democratic parties and their candidates. The 2009 presidential and parliamentary elections appeared legitimate and as free from conspiracies or election fraud as most democratic elections. Currently, the population seems to be more concerned with the economy over Islamic or security issues. Voters overwhelmingly supported the Democrat party (Partai Demokrat-PD) of President Susilo Bambang Yudhoyono (commonly referred to as SBY) over more traditional Islamic parties.[5]

A recent accomplishment includes separating the military and police, in addition to active duty military officers no longer serving dual roles in the Indonesian parliament while in uniform. However, the TNI still remains the cornerstone institution for building the country's leadership as many serving civilian government candidates come from the military.[6] Future presidents and administrations will still need to continue to work towards legitimacy and halt nepotism through the leadership positions. Reform ideas still abound from both internal and external sources, including the U.S., about how to implement more civilian control of the military.

Although the majority of Indonesians practice moderate Islam, Indonesia has AQN affiliates throughout the islands such as Jemmah Islamiya and other extremist

---

[5]Vaughn, *Indonesia* (2011), 12.

[6]Ibid.

groups like Kompak and Darul Islam.[7] Unintentionally, Indonesia has been a terrorist

safe-haven, and many analysts note the geography (with approximately 6,000 inhabited

islands and 17,000 plus total islands, spread over 1.8 million square kilometers)[8] provides

opportunity for unobservable Islamic fundamentalist growth. Islamic fundamentalists

conducted sporadic terror incidents in Indonesia over the last decade. After 9/11,

Indonesia emerged on the world stage because of the terrorist bombings in Bali in 2002,

the Marriott Hotel bombing in 2003 and more recently the bombing of twin luxury hotels

in Jakarta in 2009, all of which killed local Indonesians and Western tourists.[9]

Kopassus

As Indonesia grew into an independent country, the military's organization and

ability to control and protect the country made it the most powerful national institution.

As an archipelago, Indonesia struggled to provide for and maintain all the islands with a

national sovereign identity among the many ethnicities, tribes and religions. The TNI and

Kopassus operated under a rule called Dwifungsi, meaning it was both an external

protectorate of the country and was also charged with internal nation-building.[10] In

essence, the military protected Indonesia as it struggled to preserve its independence from

---

[7]Sydney Jones, "Are Indonesian Terror Networks Regrouping?" *BBC News*, March 10, 2010.

[8]Vaughn, *Indonesia* (2011), 1.

[9]Ibid., 23.

[10]Dana Priest, *The Mission: Waging War and Keeping the Peace with America's Military* (New York: W.W. Norton & Company, Inc., 2003), 216.

11

European or Asian powers through internal security and conduct nation-building among its numerous islands.

The Japanese controlled the islands after the Dutch during WW II and the Dutch tried to reclaim the Spice Islands after WW II. The Dutch could not support another conflict, especially far from Europe.[11] During the struggles after WWII the Dutch SOF did inflict many casualties shocking the Indonesians with their ability. These Indonesian revolutionaries realized they needed a specialized unit, with particular skills after their fight for independence from the Dutch. The military decided to form this specialized unit, which would eventually become the Kopassus.[12] Inside the TNI the Kopassus had, and continues to have, an enormous influence with many generals coming from this elite Special Forces unit.

The Kopassus originated from the Dutch Special Forces as the unit's formation came from a former Dutch officer. This Dutch Special Forces officer, Major Visser, remained after Indonesian independence and settled on the island of Java, married an Indonesian woman and changed his name.[13] Not only did he provide the training and establish the unit's baseline, he became the unit's first commander bringing with him Dutch SOF influence.

Today, the Kopassus conduct many operations throughout the islands of Indonesia. There are small elements of Kopassus located throughout the islands, based

---

[11]Ricklefs.

[12]Kenneth J. Conboy, *Kopassus: Inside Indonesia's Special Forces* (Jakarta: Equinox Publications, 2003).

[13]Ibid.

12

where the government sees fit to develop and act on intelligence to provide security for the nation. Kopassus are the primary unit used to respond to terrorist attacks and hostage rescue operations. The unit's purpose and competence in security led the Australian government to continue to train and support the Kopassus. The Australian government realized the Kopassus are the most likely unit in Indonesia to provide protection and security for visiting Australian tourists. Australian journalists have warned of Australia's SOF training with a unit accused of human rights violations. However, these arguments are balanced with understanding the need for a competent Indonesian security force, especially a counter-terror and counter-hijacking force, able to protect the many Australian citizens, diplomats and tourists found throughout the islands.[14]

Human Rights Violations

The international media constantly accuses the Indonesian security forces, police and the military of human rights violations. Numerous independent external and internal human rights groups watch every move of the Indonesian security forces and record every accusation from the populous. Many of the accusations are single-sourced and reported from convicted criminals or suspects involved in crimes. While this does not completely delegitimize their claims, it does stand to reason that not all claims are creditable. Sometimes vengeful claims from arrested parties may receive undue attention piled on an institution already labeled guilty of past atrocities. The balance of investigating true versus vengeful claims is difficult to say the least. The Kopassus and TNI are praised by the Indonesian government as well as other security forces for their

---

[14]Allan Behm, "Cooperation With Kopassus? Take Care!" *Agenda* 10, no. 1 (2003): 13-18.

efficiency in man-hunting criminals and terrorists in the lens of tactical prowess. Accomplishing the same effect while adhering to due process of law and observing human rights is the goal for any government's security force. Balancing the change of the tactics, which are criticized by human rights groups, while keeping up the same effectiveness in operations, is a difficult task to be sure. One that might need additional U.S. SOF consultation, oversight and patience to address.

Throughout its history, Indonesia dealt with what was internally considered an uprising for independence from activists in the provinces of Papua, Aceh, and East Timor.[15] The TNI and the Kopassus were repeatedly accused of human rights violations in the response to these "uprisings." The history with East Timor is the most recognizable of these events, as the country eventually gained independence from Indonesia and is recognized as a completely separate country. Officially, in 2002 East Timor became a sovereign state after a long drawn out struggle with Indonesia.[16]

Starting in 1975, East Timor (also commonly referred to as Timor-Leste) attempted to legally become an independent state and separate from Indonesia. The majority of East Timorese resisted integration with Indonesia.[17] The Kopassus formed pro-Indonesian militias to quell the independence movement. For close to 25 years, the TNI and Kopassus conducted many operations, building these militias and conducting unilateral activities to carry out killings, kidnappings and sabotage. The number of casualties and displaced persons from these operations vary between organizations and

---

[15]Vaughn, *Indonesia* (2011), 13.

[16]Ibid., 14.

[17]Ibid.

14

reports. The numbers of dead range up to one third of the East Timor population over the

years due to fighting and famine as a result of the conflict, with hundreds of thousands

displaced. Of note, in 1999 after a vote for independence Indonesian forces along with

pro-integrationist militias killed approximately 7,000 and around 300,000 displaced from

the East Timorese. The TNI were fearful that independence for East Timor could set off a

chain reaction to other islands and regions, which also had issue with the central

Indonesian government and try to separate as well.[18]

U.S. Policy

The U.S. must continually evaluate the balance of Western ideals and values

versus the strategic value of a partnership with a given country. The U.S. is a beacon of

freedom and democracy for the world, and while the U.S. tries to export both, sometimes

the expectation for other countries to meet Western standards impedes the progress of

that relationship. The U.S. relationship with Indonesia is a prime example of imposing

the Western standards for governmental and security forces progression on a developing

country.

Since the atrocities of East Timor in 1999, U.S. foreign policy over the last

decade towards Indonesia prevented much in-depth interaction with the Indonesian

military or TNI. The U.S. government followed the Leahy Conditions and refused to give

security-related foreign assistance to a military, which failed to observe human rights or

prosecute those accused.[19] In 2005, the Bush administration softened the restrictions and

---

[18]Ibid.

[19]Charles Comer, "Leahy in Indonesia: Damned if You Do (and Even if you Don't," *Asian Affairs: An American Review* 37 (2010).

reestablished a limited engagement with the TNI in an effort to build a regional partner for the war on terror.[20] However full U.S. Special Forces integration or embedding with the Kopassus was not allowed under these rules.

In November 2010 President Barack Obama made a point to stop in Indonesia early on after taking office, where he commented about the importance of an alliance with Indonesia.[21] As of 2012, the Obama administration allowed the U.S. Mission to Indonesia to initiate "a gradual and measured program of cooperative activities" with the Kopassus.[22] As of this thesis, that program only included the plan for a non-lethal Joint Combined Exchange Training (commonly referred to as a JCET, pronounced Jay-Set), with no date, training priority or actual unit specified.[23]

China

When writing about any country in the Asia-Pacific rim aspects of the influence of China should be researched as well. Certain decisions a country makes might seem counter-intuitive or misunderstood without weighing in the effects of China on that country or the region. China is emerging as the closest near-peer superpower for the United States. Smaller countries throughout the Asia-Pacific region weigh their policy decisions based on how those decisions will effect relations between both the U.S. and China. Indonesia must contend with this perceived competition as well, caught between

---

[20]Ibid.

[21]Ibid., 65.

[22]US Mission to Indonesia, FY 2013 Mission Strategic and Resource Plan, 28.

[23]Defense Attaché's Office, E-mail exchanges between members and author, November 2012 to April 2013.

16

China and the U.S. both of which realize the need for an improved relationship with this key Southeast Asian nation.

China's influence is growing, not only in the Asia-Pacific region, but also throughout the world. Theorists argue about Chinese intentions with this rising influence. Many analysts focus only on China as a possible near-peer military competitor and the next emerging super-power along the same vein as views of the former U.S.S.R rather than as a potential partner. The U.S. Department of Defense keeps a watchful eye on the evolution of the Chinese military, and their worldwide engagements. This raises questions about U.S. strategy possibly trying to contain China's spread or race for resources and-or allies. Only China can reveal its true intentions, on its own or through future U.S. diplomatic engagement. However, Indonesia presents some unique dynamics for both the U.S. and China with their respective national interests, which could have global impacts.

China does not have the same moral lens as the U.S. and may become a viable alternative to Southeast Asian partner forces in the absence of a strong U.S. military relationship. As a regional power, without a U.S. presence, China becomes the most prominent power for any of the smaller Asian nations. Prominent not only in military relationships, but China also rises in power for economic trade and regional stability.

The South China Sea dispute highlights the many ways China will attempt to gain power in the region. Southeast Asia, especially the bordering states of the South China Sea are a valuable area for China. The Malacca Straits, which are located between Indonesia, Malaysia and Singapore, provide exclusive access to the South China Sea trade routes. The media generally highlights that China must be after natural resources in

17

their pursuit as there are oil and natural gas fields in the South China Sea; however control and influence are just as important.[24] Expanding China's security buffer by controlling more area provides China more advantages than the small amount of actual energy resources located in the South China Sea. If China gains influence over the ASEAN countries, especially a stronger influence than the U.S., the buffer of protection surrounding China increases dramatically. Additionally, there are economic gains for China's own GDP by having more influence over the ASEAN states, as well as increasing its trade partners. Indonesia is a key element in this concept for not only the obvious geographical location, but for the countries it can influence and the symbolic representation as an ally.

Definitions

This thesis was written during the Command and General Staff College course year 2012 to 2013, therefore "current" in regards to strategy, situations or any other references are regarded to be in the realm of 2005 to 2013. The author chose 2005 because of the Bush administration's decision to reengage with Indonesia (not Kopassus) following full disengagement in the late 1990s.

Throughout the thesis, when referring to Southeast Asia the nations of ASEAN are generally understood to be the countries. Since Indonesia borders the southern portion of the South China Sea, the author chose to include all of the ASEAN states because of Indonesia's ability or opportunity to influence or operate in any of them. There are

---

[24]Aileen S. P. Baviera, *The South China Sea Territorial Disputes in ASEAN-China Relations*, http://nghiencuubiendong.vn/download/doc_download/377-aileen-sp-baviera-the-south-china-sea-territorial-disputes-in-asean-china-relations (accessed April 18, 2013).

currently 10 nations in ASEAN: Indonesia, Malaysia, the Philippines, Singapore, Thailand, Brunei, Myanmar (Burma), Cambodia, Laos, and Vietnam.

Limitations

A limitation encountered during the research of this thesis was the political reasoning for withholding engagement from the Kopassus even after the repeal of the Leahy Conditions. The Bush administration began to reengage with the Indonesian military in 2005. In 2010, the Obama administration specifically addressed the need to reengage with the Kopassus with Secretary of Defense Gates announcement the U.S. would resume engagement. While all signs pointed toward reengagement, there was still administration resistance for undisclosed reasons. SOF JCETs were planned, resourced and prepared to execute, but were never given the go ahead by the U.S. Mission in Indonesia. The author's research led to key individuals in the upper-levels of the administration withholding the decision to engage but no concrete reasons were available to the author. The exploration of this resistance included e-mail exchanges with analysts in the Office of the Secretary of Defense, the Defense Attaché's Office in Jakarta, Indonesia and other Southeast Asian analysts working for the U.S. DoD. An attitude of "not right now" became prevalent among those working below upper level decision makers with no specific justification for the continued disengagement.

Another limitation was the original plan for interviews with analysts and planners from the interagency community and DoD. The idea was in the process however, budget constraints prevented any attempt to travel for interviews; therefore, the research was communicated through e-mail or phone conversations.

<u>Delimitations</u>

A delimitation of this thesis is an examination of human rights violations prosecutions in the TNI, Kopassus or other countries around the world. The data may have been available for comparison to show prosecution and punishment of Kopassus members specifically for human rights violations, but there was no readily available repository for use. Additionally, to prove or disprove the Leahy Conditions effects, one would have to prove the Indonesian government prosecuted Kopassus members because the violations were illegal in Indonesia. If the Indonesian government prosecuted accused members solely because the U.S. imposed the Leahy Conditions, and thus denied funding, one would have to examine if that met the intent of the conditions in the first place.

While it is obvious through the research that the prosecutions of individuals so far is unsatisfactory in the eyes of internal and external human rights organizations, it is not obvious if the prosecutions have been reasonably conducted in the eyes of the U.S. government. Additionally, if a comparison was made related to other countries the U.S. imposed the Leahy Conditions upon; the data might point to equal or unequal implementation of the laws. An examination of the Leahy Conditions application and repeal with regards to Indonesia would be a whole thesis by itself, as relevant as it would be to this particular research.

Summary

U.S. policy makers and senior military commanders already plan reengagement for the Kopassus. The issue of whether that engagement is right or wrong is irrelevant for a military author. It will happen. The issue now is the best use of the U.S. military instrument of power to improve the relationship with Indonesia. While U.S. SOF is not the answer for everything, nor should it be, a SOF-to-SOF relationship with the Kopassus can provide more than a competent SOF partner element. Because of how important and influential the Kopassus is to the Indonesian government a long-term partnership, fully integrated, can build relationships and promote U.S. values. These relationships will be built with the current leadership and more importantly the future leaders of not just the military, but the likely future policy makers for the country.

The U.S. will have to be more selective with its engagement of foreign partners, with budget constraints and a reduction in forces. Which countries will receive shorter duration training engagements, senior leader dialogues, and which few may establish full partner forces with the U.S. need to be prioritized. The prioritization will come from where the U.S. can have the greatest impact for the amount of resources put against an engagement objective. A country with great influence and importance to a region, which can also influence neighboring countries, and possibly unilaterally conduct security operations throughout a region, would be a high priority country. Indonesia appears to fit that description in the Asian Pacific rim as a whole, and especially in Southeast Asia. Finding where the U.S. can invest the least resources, in this case through the use of the military instrument of power, but retain the greatest impact is a logical and fiscally responsible concept. The following chapters will help to research, define and recommend answers to this concept.

A review of the literature conducted in chapter 2 will examine the influence Indonesia exerts in the Southeast Asian region. Chapter 3 explains the research methodology used for the development of this recommendation. The analysis of the research is presented in chapter 4. Finally, chapter 5 presents Conclusions and Recommendations for the greatest national interest gain with the least investment. Understanding the importance of the Kopassus is key to realizing the best method for U.S. engagement in Indonesia. Contemporary journalists, policy makers, and officially sanctioned reports will show the importance of the Kopassus to Indonesia, as well as Indonesia in the Asian-Pacific as demonstrated in a thorough literature review.

CHAPTER 2

LITERATURE REVIEW

Introduction

A thorough Literature Review is organized with research grouped by subject to provide well-rounded coverage of the issues discussed. In the first subheading, Overview of Indonesia will lay the groundwork for why the country is important to U.S. policy. Throughout the overview the reader is exposed to Indonesia's importance in Southeast Asia. The research focused on Indonesia's general description, small amounts of pertinent history, and development. In the next subheading, TNI and Kopassus, both contemporary and historical authors show the importance of the military in the country. The value of the TNI to the country of Indonesia's relatively recent development as a democratic government is apparent throughout the readings. Additionally the formation of the Kopassus is laid out as it progressed over time. A synopsis of the U.S. administrations sentiments towards reengagement with the Kopassus is covered as well.

In Southeast Asia no country can operate without considering China's actions. Therefore the subheading of China covers Indonesia's importance to China. Recent issues in the region, between not only Indonesia and China but also other Southeast Asian nations as well.

Because the Kopassus and TNI are most recognized because of human rights violations, they are covered in the next subheading Human Rights Violations. The history associated with these violations from a historical context as well as contemporary authors and organizations dedicated to pursuing those accused are covered. Significant amounts of articles are written in response to both the TNI's committing of human rights and the

23

resultant evolution of U.S. policies towards Indonesia. These articles and reports provided a look at the world's view of the Kopassus and their involvement in numerous human rights violations.

As the thesis is about U.S. policy, the final subheading for chapter 2 is appropriately titled U.S. Strategy—Policy in Indonesia—Pivot to the Pacific. This section contains a short overview of some history behind the U.S.'s engagements. Mostly contemporary authors, reports and speeches show the recent administrations of both Bush and Obama promoting a renewed relationship with Indonesia. The USPACOM commander's testimony before the House Armed Services Committee provides a well-timed focus relevant to this thesis.

Post 9/11, many analysts advocated both for and against the restart and integration of Indonesia's Kopassus military-to-military relationship with the United States. For the purposes of this thesis, the reader must understand how important the Kopassus are as an organization in the Indonesian military and government.

Overview of Indonesia

A History of Modern Indonesia since c. 1300, by M. C. Ricklefs looks into the early introduction of Islam to the islands in Southeast Asia. This book helped to realize the historical importance for Islamic fundamentalists in conducting operations in Indonesia. Understanding Indonesia's past is the value of this book, which provides insight into the potential of AQN continuing to operate in Indonesia given its historical linkage to the spread of Islam. Ricklefs covers Indonesian history from circa 1300 through 1975 in the President Suharto era.

This book provided a good, quick overview of how the Dutch colonized the islands for spices. Then, because of WW II and global commitments, the Dutch departed and the Japanese invaded. After WW II, the Indonesians confiscated Japanese weapons to defend themselves and were able to repulse the Dutch from retaking the island chains. The post-WWII timeframe, where the Dutch were too weak to retake the islands, provided Indonesia its first opportunity to become an independent nation-state.

Due to the damage inflicted by the Dutch, the often-opposing ethnicities and smaller island tribes of Indonesia unified to fight a common enemy in the Dutch occupation. While there were many different groups in modern Indonesia wanting their individual independence, during this revolution they were able to moderately unify to fight for common independence from a European enemy.

A similarly named book, History of Modern Indonesia, written by Adrian Vickers, again shows how Indonesia found its independence from a long period of Dutch rule. The book seeks to help the reader understand the foundation of the Indonesian government and its subsequent three-decade plus rule under President Suharto. Vickers sets the stage for why the country found itself as a religious battleground where terrorists could find safe-haven and execute bombings. The book also helps to establish all that is Indonesia, the demography, geography, population, religious influential leaders and the importance in the world.

Vickers is very factual and explains the greater significance of how large and diverse Indonesia is with its 17,000 plus islands, 6,000 plus of them inhabited. This book was used more as a confirmation of facts and data to show the relevance of Indonesia in Southeast Asia, especially with regards to size both in land mass area and populace.

The Congressional Research Service provides policy and legal analysis for both the House and the Senate as well as to specific committees. Bruce Vaughn, titled as a Specialist in Asian Affairs, has written and continually updated Indonesia: Domestic Politics, Strategic Dynamics, and U.S. Interests. Vaughn's most recent work, dated January 31, 2011 provides a wealth of information on the demography, geography, and political background, role of the military, movements including the secessionist movements, economy, foreign policy and U.S.-Indonesia relations. The report assisted in gaining an understanding of the synopsis overview and recommendations, which Vaughn gave to U.S. policy makers in 2011. This thesis used the baseline line information on the most current trends, attitudes or outlooks in Indonesia from Vaughn's research.

The Congressional Research Service report is a fantastic overview of all salient details with regard to Indonesia and any issues or involvement with the United States. Vaughn captures the facts as well as puts general analysis and predominant opinions throughout his report. The report contains a series of well written synopsis of the general history of the country, the general history of the politics, the general history of the secessionist movements of provinces including East Timor and the general history of U.S. policy and relations between the last two administrations. Any author would do well to refer to these reports to gain a baseline understanding of Indonesia especially as it relates to the United States.

TNI and Kopassus

Again, Bruce Vaughn's "Indonesia: Domestic Politics, Strategic Dynamics, and U.S. Interests" provides a well written synopsis of the overview of the Indonesian military and situation with regards to the relationship with the United States. Vaughn

26

covers the idea for attempts by both the Bush and Obama administrations to reconnect with Indonesia. Especially in regards to the military-to-military relationship, Vaughn highlights how former President Bush's administration worked to reinitiate the relationship through International Military Education and Training (known as IMET), Foreign Military Financing (FMF) and Foreign Military Sales (FMS). The importance for a relationship with Indonesia to the Bush administration appeared obvious as the U.S. executed the Global War on Terror and AQN affiliates conducted attacks in Indonesia in the early 2000s.

The Obama administration continued to rekindle the relationship with Indonesia. Vaughn notes that President Obama's visit was highly anticipated and very well received in Jakarta. As a former resident of Jakarta, Obama even spoke Indonesian during a speech, positively rallying the population. Coupled with then Secretary of Defense Robert Gates 2010 visit and statements about the importance of the mutual relationship, Vaughn sees the tide of Indonesian public opinion shifting toward a more pro-U.S. sentiment.

For a look at the creation of the Kopassus, the book by Ken Conboy titled *Kopassus: Inside Indonesia's Special Forces*, provided the establishment and initial leadership for the unit. The book addresses the history of the creation of the Kopassus from within the Indonesian military from 1952 to 1993. The author lived in Indonesia for many years and published the book in Jakarta. Not only does the book describe in detail the beginning leadership, which sets the stage for the attitude and vision of the organization, but also reveals how junior leadership from the Kopassus become influential throughout Indonesia in later years. Many of the junior officers throughout

Kopassus early years rise to the rank of general officer and become commanders of large formations/commands in the TNI.

An interesting perspective from this book is how the damage Dutch Special Forces inflicted on the Indonesians during the revolution caused the Kopassus precursor units formation. The violence these smaller units were able to execute against lesser-trained revolutionaries caught the attention of the Indonesians. The guerrilla fighters who survived understood what it would take to counter this type of force in the future and immediately recognized the need for a specialized selection and training program beyond that of a conscripted army.

A fascinating discovery in Conboy's book is the original unit, training pipeline, and establishment of the founding doctrine and tactics, techniques and procedures originated from a former Dutch Special Forces officer. Major Rokus Visser married a local woman and changed his name to Mohamad Idjon Djanbi while living and working in Indonesia. Visser became a peaceful, law-abiding citizen in Indonesia. After the Indonesian military leaders who wanted to establish this new special operations unit sought out Visser, he easily agreed to begin the training.

This Dutch Special Forces influence reveals to the reader how connected Indonesia still is to the era of Dutch colonial rule. This influence remains today, as the Kopassus still wear the Red Beret, which Visser established for the designation based on the Dutch Red Beret. Visser even acted as the Kopassus' first commander.

The unit's mission broadened to a wide range of special operations including; direct action, unconventional warfare, sabotage, counter-insurgency, counter-terrorism, and intelligence gathering. The intelligence gathering influence came from the

Indonesian military leader who originally sought to create the unit, Colonel Alexander

Evert Kawilarang. Col Kawilarang and the unit he came from had a strong focus on

intelligence gathering, as a sort of military intelligence unit. This aspect remains a part of

the organization's mission, even as after the change from operating under Dwifungsi.

This abandonment of the concept of Dwifungsi is widely accepted as Indonesia

transitioned to civilian control of the military.[25]

It is important to highlight that the name of the Kopassus changed over the years.

Originally, the unit was designated as Kesatuan Komando Tentara Territorium

III/Siliwangi, then Third Territorial Command: Komando Teritorium Tiga (KTT), then

Korps Komando, Angkatan Darat (KKAD), Resimen Para Komando Angkatan Darat

(RPKAD), and Kopasandha. Conboy covers these developments in detail. This is

important to note for historical context as the attribution for certain operations will

identify these other unit names but are the same as the current Kopassus. The term

Kopassus comes from the combination of the Indonesian words *KOmando PASukan*

khuSUS, meaning the Army Special Forces Command.

The unit grew over its history from one company of approximately 100 soldiers to

five regiments totaling upwards of 5,000 soldiers.[26] The units have different specialties as

they have grown over the years to compliment each other's operations. The groups

specialize as follows: Group 1 and 2—Special Operation forces, Jungle warfare,

Unconventional Warfare, Counter-Insurgency, Special Reconnaissance, and Direct

---

[25]Conboy.

[26]Ibid.

29

Action. Group 3—Combat Intelligence, Group 4—Training, and Group 5 (also known as unit 81)—Counter Terrorism.[27]

Chapter 20 of Conboy's book covers a developing time for the Kopassus in the 1980s and 1990s. This is a critical time of reform as it highlights how Indonesia's leadership rejected the U.S. and instead preferred to imitate the British. It is of note that the Indonesian Minister of Defense during this timeframe was a former Kopassus member, showing the influence the unit maintains. This Minister of Defense had no issue rejecting the U.S. even as the U.S.S.R. collapsed leaving the U.S. as the world's lone super-power. The Kopassus reorganized under a model fashioned after the British SAS in their organization and training.

Many authors talk about the Indonesian military concept they originally operated under during the famed Suharto 30 year rule. The concept of "Dwifungsi," the dual function for the Indonesian military to operate as both internal and external security is an important point covered by many authors. Dana Priest's book, The Mission, captured this well during the research. The most important point for this concept to be understood in the Indonesian culture was that Indonesia was facing internal threats more than external threats. Therefore the military acted in a policing role inside the many territories. What makes this even more significant for Indonesia is how one has to look at the country's geography. As a large archipelago, one island's instability was essentially an internal threat to the greater Indonesia. This would literally require the deployment of troops off the mainland of the island of Java to counter or control the threat. Additionally, the administration stationed troops on different islands to enforce the laws. The Kopassus'

---

[27]Ibid.

role in this would usually be to deploy, calm the violence, hunt the rebels with orders to kill/capture the leadership, and then allow the greater TNI to come in, clean-up and conduct internal nation-building type activities.

Generally, the rest of the world frowns on the concept of using a nations' military to enforce internal stability. However, Indonesia's geography and developing national unity led to the need for military employment on other islands to develop the nation. Until a professional police force could be developed on most inhabited islands, the nation's central authority for enforcement of laws was the military.

China

There is an historical aspect of China and Indonesia's relationship that must be understood. Namely, there is a critical segment of the population known as Chinese Indonesians who are typically either rich business and property owners or poor and considered a drain on the system.[28] Over the years, there have been many incidents of discrimination against this vulnerable, marginalized Chinese Indonesian population.

The Indonesia Reader: History, Culture, Politics by Tineke and Hellwig gives an overview of the Chinese in Indonesia. These Chinese have bounced back and forth dealing with discrimination because of their ethnicity and religion (most are Buddhists or Christian). In the late 1990s, the government introduced laws to protect the indigenous Chinese in Indonesia. Unfortunately, anti-Chinese riots followed as the Indonesian population believed rich Chinese bought off local politicians to benefit from the laws.

---

[28]Tineke Hellwig and Eric Tagliacozzo, eds., *The Indonesia Reader: History, Culture, Politics* (Durham, NC: Duke University Press, 2009).

In *A History of Modern Indonesia since c. 1300*, by M.C. Ricklefs, and Robert Cribb's, '*The Indonesian Marxist tradition*,' both authors review Indonesia's history with communism. This historical aspect must be understood as Indonesia went through its forming in the post World-War II days under their first President Sukarno. After President Sukarno came to power, there was a warming of the relationship between communist China, the Soviet Union and Indonesia. Sukarno associated anything "Western" with the past exploitation of Indonesia by the Dutch colonials. This caused a belief that a relationship with the capitalist U.S. could regress Indonesia into a subservient role. Interestingly, the introduction of early communist ideas originated with Dutch socialists who tried to help the Indonesians resist Dutch colonial rule.[29]

It was during this formative time that Indonesia viewed China's communist government as a better form to follow. Cribb and Ricklefs overview how Indonesia associated with China for a brief time to learn about communist governing while at the same-time the U.S. pushed a containment strategy against the spread of communism. This background was used to analyze the historical connection China has with Indonesia as both were developing into their modern government systems. The depth of Ricklef's book in covering the early history provides interesting information relevant for understanding Indonesia's history. However, too much of the book focused on the history prior to the 1990s to be of relevance to contemporary issues facing the U.S. in Indonesia.

In the Congressional Research Service report by Bruce Vaughn, he covers the rise of the Communist Party of Indonesia, the PKI, during the 1950s. During this time, the

---

[29]Robert Cribb, "The Indonesian Marxist tradition," in *Marxism in Asia*, eds., C. P. Mackerras and N. J. Knight (London: Croom Helm, 1985), 251-272.

U.S. surreptitiously supported rebellious military activities as part of the containment of communism. It was during this time that the military took over power in Indonesia, as some describe, to prevent the communists from taking power. Some believe that General Suharto, Indonesia's ruler for over 30 years, directed the crisis to take power for himself and his followers. The relationship between the U.S. with Indonesia was sporadic at this time. The concept of preventing the spread of communism was in line with the U.S. strategy of the day; however, there were hundreds of thousands of deaths during this time. As Indonesia was going through a time of anti-Communist purges and rebellious riots, the government overly crushed any rivalry, especially one associated with communism. China saw some good relations with the PKI, and many in Indonesia saw China's version of a socialist communist state a better alternative.

Contemporary articles highlight the engagement strategy of the U.S. in the South China Sea region. Richard N. Haass writing in *Foreign Affairs* discusses the rebalancing of American policy towards Asia in his May-June 2013 article "The Irony of American Strategy." In this article, Haass points out the importance of balancing the U.S.-China relations as China rises in power and exerts more influence in the South China Sea. Haass begins the article talking about the Middle East and how the U.S. cannot leave or actually Pivot away from the region. For more than just the decade of war, as the U.S. has been integrally involved in the Middle East. The biggest point Haass makes is that the U.S. has been a lone super power since the fall of the U.S.S.R. but failed to focus on a long term strategy, until 9/11.

While analyzing China, Haass compliments the administration's efforts to move resources and focus to the Pacific region. Haass describes how the entire region's stability, not only economically, but also militarily depends on a good U.S.-China relationship. Smaller countries throughout the region will be hedging their alliances between China and the United States. The U.S. focus should be to ensure that China cannot or does not choose to act aggressively.

China sees the value in a strong partnership with Indonesia as China pushes to gain control over the South China Sea. Many journalists claim China's interest in the South China Sea is over natural resources. However, according to the U.S. Energy Information Administration, report on the South China Sea the resources are minimal compared to the rest of the world's supply. While China's conflict over the territorial lines of control of the South China Sea mostly involve Vietnam, the Philippines, Brunei and Malaysia, according to the '9 dashed line' claim of China, Indonesia's oil fields are affected as well.[30]

Human Rights Violations

For a look into the human rights violations, this thesis will analyze many articles by modern authors. Particularly specific to this course of research are articles from Human Rights Watch. "'What did I do Wrong?' Papuans in Merauke Face Abuses by Indonesian Special Forces" provides insight to firsthand accounts from victims of these human rights violations. With a look at six specific case studies, and a summary of the Kopassus type of abuses, this article purports that the unit randomly kidnaps people who may have been near an incident in the local community and beats, tortures and

---

[30]US Energy Information Administration, *South China Sea Full Report*, February 7, 2013, http://www.eia.gov/countries/regions-topics.cfm?fips=SCS (accessed April 15, 2013).

relentlessly questions them. The abuses appear to have similarities in techniques used and situations resulting in the peoples kidnappings. The article culminates with suggestions for the U.S., the international community and the Indonesian government to correct the abuses.

The suggestions from this Human Rights Watch article for the Indonesian government focus on investigations by impartial committees, protection of civilians from retaliation and prosecution of the violators found guilty. Further, Human Rights Watch recommends the U.S. and the international community withholds training and funding from the Kopassus and encourages the Indonesian government to take action.[31]

The East Timor Action Network (seen on other websites referred to as ETAN) provides coverage on human rights violations and keeps a continual website and blog up for advertising and publicizing the latest information with regard to actions of the U.S. government in dealing with Indonesia. ETAN is adamantly against any support of the Indonesian military, and especially the Kopassus until there is full prosecution for all soldiers implicated in human rights abuses. The unnamed author cites that he was just looking into photos of abuses in East Timor and while there was no definitive proof that Kopassus was involved, he was sure of they were.[32] The article continues to vent its disappointment and "disgust" with U.S. policy for planning to reengage with the Kopassus or meet with its leaders. The website also contains a blog (tab) for the West

---

[31]Human Rights Watch, "What Did I Do Wrong? Papauans in Merauke Face Abuses by Indonesian Special Forces," June 2009, http://www.hrw.org/reports/2009/06/25/what-did-i-do-wrong (accessed November 14, 2012).

[32]East Timor Action Network, "Secretary of Defense Gates Goes to Jakarta Bearing Kopassus Gift," http://etanaction.blogspot.com/2010/07/secretary-of-gate-goes-to-jakarta.html (accessed April 14, 2013).

Papua Advocacy Team (referred to between the groups as WPAT), a fellow human rights website specifically set up to monitor human rights abuses and prosecution of abusers.

An article from The Australian.com, US resumes ties with Indonesia's Kopassus special forces, despite its past writes in detail about what the SECDEF, other regional experts and opposing activists say about Kopassus. The article highlights that the new relationship was because of progress by the Indonesian government and military made in reference to reforms.[33] An activist in the article, Usman Hamid makes the claim that the U.S. must be weary of reestablishing a relationship with Kopassus until the violators of human rights are removed completely from the Indonesian military.[34]

Another article found on the Human Rights Watch website, "Indonesia: US Resumes Military Assistance to Abusive Force," criticizes the Obama administration for lifting the ban on the Kopassus. The article explains the criteria Secretary Gates gave to the Indonesian government to resume the military-to-military relationship. Specifically, the Indonesian government and the Kopassus must remove convicted personnel from the Special Forces, pledge cooperation with investigations and prosecutions, and prohibit convicted persons and suspend credibly accused violators from serving. Human Rights Watch does not agree that these criteria are strict enough, nor believe they will be

---

[33]Australian News, "US Resumes Ties with Indonesia's Kopassus Special Forces, Despite Its Past." July 22, 2010, http://www.theaustralian.com.au/national-affairs/opinion/friendly-china-ups-ante-in-cyber-warfare/story-e6frgd0x-1226654075003 (accessed January 5, 2013).

[34]Ibid.

enforced.[35] This article helped to identify the opposition to the reestablishment of a relationship with the Kopassus. An analysis of the Indonesian military justice system provides this thesis with an understanding of why Human Rights Watch suspects the Indonesian military will not comply with the stipulations the U.S. seeks to impose. This article provided the researcher the view for the opposition's arguments against improving the relationship with the Kopassus.

Following President Obama's visit in 2010, *Asian Affairs: An American Review*, published an article examining the Leahy laws with regard to the Kopassus. Specifically, the article explains the creation and purpose of the Leahy laws and their applicability to Indonesia and the Kopassus. Leahy in "Indonesia: Damned if You Do (and Even if You Don't)" covers well the Presidents dilemma of easing the Leahy Laws on a unit and country that has made minor gains in improving its accountability of human rights violations. Written by Charles "Ken" Comer, the article is critical of the U.S. administration for applying these laws inconsistently and indifferently.

Another contemporary article on Australian SOF and government support for the Kopassus provided a perspective on the effectiveness of the Kopassus with regards to countering terrorism. Allan Behm wrote in his article that balancing protection of Australia's interests, specifically its embassy, tourists and citizens living abroad, with partnering with a force accused of human rights violations. "Cooperation With Kopassus? Take Care!," published in *Agenda* Volume 10 in 2003, highlights the importance of the Australian Special Air Service Regiment ensuring that Australian interests are protected

---

[35]Human Rights Watch, "Indonesia: US Resumes Military Assistance to Abusive Force," July 22, 2010, http://www.hrw.org/news/2010/07/22/indonesia-us-resumes-military-assistance-abusive-force (accessed January 5, 2013).

in Indonesia while cautioning against supporting a SOF unit that may or may not be under the control of the Indonesian government.

Behm makes the point that the Australian government realizes to deal with the Indonesian military is to deal with Kopassus officers. As Kopassus officers populate the highest ranks of the Indonesian military, to try to ignore them based on affiliation with their past unit would be impossible to deal with the military.

U.S. Strategy—Policy in Indonesia—Pivot to the Pacific

A key document analyzed in this research is the plan for the U.S. Mission to Indonesia. Published by the Department of State, a Sensitive but Unclassified version of the FY 2013 Mission Strategic and Resource Plan reveals the exact U.S. policy towards Indonesia and sheds light on U.S. expectations, funding and requirements for improving the military-to-military relationship. Addressed specifically in one of the ten goals for the Mission is engagement with the Kopassus with established criteria. Goal number six, under Facilitating Reform of Security Forces/CT Efforts and Addressing Transnational Organized Crime. In the goal, the Mission addresses being a reliable partner with Indonesian forces. The goal only explains the Mission has initiated a measured program of cooperative activities. The goal covers the ideas that the U.S. and Indonesia have worked well toward security issues in the past especially in light of Indonesia's response to terrorist attacks. The Mission states the U.S. needs to rebuild its relationship, reducing suspicion from Indonesia that the U.S. is an unreliable partner because of limited interaction.

In a professional Army officer publication by the Association of the U.S. Army, the United States Army Torchbearer National Security Report for April 2013 covers The

US Army in the Pacific: Assuring Security and Stability. The publication lists Indonesia several times for engagement as both a joint exercise partner and for senior leader engagement. A highlight and theme throughout the entire publication is that the key to future security challenges is building cooperation with America's allies and partnering with capable militaries throughout the region. One of the articles discusses that coalitions need to be fostered early on, not last minute during times of crisis. These types of coalition relationships take time to build and can be enriched with trust which is only gained through time and experience.

Political Islam in Southeast Asia: Moderates, Radicals and Terrorists by Angel Rabasa is a short synopsis of how the terrorist threat in Southeast Asia evolved. Published in 2003 the book provides a look at how the world saw Indonesia post 9/11 when international terrorism was fresh on the minds of most, and AQN had motivated attacks in Bali and elsewhere.

Are Indonesian terror networks regrouping? from the BBC News, Jakarta, written by Karishma Vaswani is a short article linking a recent counter-terrorism unit's operational success with the possibility of a new terror conglomerate. Vaswani first reports on a raid that killed an Indonesian most wanted terrorist, named Dulmatin, who was a supplier of weapons and funding, otherwise known as the "Genius of Jemaah Islamiah." The article then suggests elements of the terror groups Jemmah Islamiya, Kompak and Darul Islam could have linked together to try to become Indonesia's new Al-Qaeda. The author suggests the fundamentalist elements in these terror groups have grown tired of inaction by their respective parent organization. These off-shoots may have formed a new element operating in the Aceh region of Indonesia.[36]

The article covers a raid against Dulmatin on a remote part of Aceh, on an alleged militant training camp. Vaswani reports that many experts believe this means networks of locals supported the camp.[37] The article quotes local government officials who admit there are radicals still in Indonesia promoting radical ideologies, but they are the exception, not the norm.[38] This thesis used this article to analyze the possibility of a growing threat in Indonesia as evidence that a partnership with the Kopassus and the TNI is important to U.S. National Security objectives. The article provided a new avenue for research into the training camps location and its importance to AQN. Future research could examine other terrorist related groups like Kompak and Darul Islam and their role in recent terrorist events.

A few articles that address the recent U.S. policy decision to remove the complete ban of working with the Kopassus shed light on the details of the ban and its current state. The majority of these articles highlight a July 2010 announcement by former Secretary of Defense (SECDEF) Robert Gates to allow a gradual program of security cooperation activities with the Kopassus.

A key and well timed review of the U.S. perspective for Indonesia came from a review of Admiral Samuel Locklear's March 2013 testimony before the House Armed

---

[36]Karishma Vaswani, "Are Indonesian terror networks regrouping?," *BBC News*, 10 March 2010, http://news.bbc.co.uk/2/hi/asia-pacific/8557561.stm (accessed January 5, 2013).

[37]Ibid.

[38]Ibid.

40

Services Committee on USPACOM posture. The testimony covers the entire USPACOM area of responsibility, from California to India. Rather than re-script the opening of the testimony a simple quote shows how the USPACOM commander summarizes—Why is the Indo-Asia-Pacific Important?

> The nations of the Indo-Asia-Pacific include five of our nation's seven treaty allies, three of the largest economies in the world, and seven of the ten smallest; the most populous nations in the world, the largest democracy; the largest Muslim-majority nation; and the world's smallest republic.[39]

Prior to that short summary, Admiral Locklear described the geographic size of the area, discussing distances and mass unequaled in other AOR's. He further describes the many militaries, sizes, sophistication and the growing of nuclear-armed or powered nations, and those pursuing nuclear power in the region. Worth mentioning among the statistics are; seven of the ten largest militaries and the largest most sophisticated navies in the world. In short, the first two pages of the testimony awe the receiver into understanding the metrics of how large, varied, diverse and difficult the USPACOM AOR is and the responsibility placed on his command. The testimony covers each of the countries throughout the AOR and describes the general concept of how USPACOM had success in the last year and how the command intends to engage in the future.

Specifically, the admiral discusses Indonesia, and the progress made by the TNI and the Kopassus. In this section, Admiral Locklear describes the plan for reengagement with the Kopassus. In this description, he states that the engagement will remain at a steady pace measured against the progress of transparency developing within the TNI and

---

[39]Statement of Admiral Samuel J. Locklear, US Navy, Commander, US Pacific Command, before the House Armed Services Committee, March 5, 2013, http://docs.house.gov/meetings/AS/AS00/20130305/100393/HHRG-113-AS00-Wstate-LocklearUSNA-20130305.pdf (accessed April 2, 2013).

Kopassus. More specifically toward the actual military-to-military engagement, the Admiral says that they will only conduct key leader dialogue and small subject matter expert exchanges in what is described as only planning and non-lethal activities. Specifically one of these activities will be education in law of war/human rights.[40] Following the paragraph about the Kopassus is a description of military trade with Indonesia.

Another key part of the USPACOM testimony is the coverage of China and the attitude the Admiral puts forth. While discussing China, the Admiral is careful to view the country as another opportunity for engagement. Viewing China as another rivalry will cause more issues, and Admiral Locklear is quite pointed in presenting a non-threatening attitude, while still standing strong on U.S. response to illegal activities in the AOR.[41]

The Literature Review covered all pertinent topics for this thesis. Broad enough to cover a general history of Indonesia for the unfamiliar, the documents reviewed provided the history associated with the focus of the thesis. As the crux of the thesis is about the influence of the TNI, more specifically the Kopassus, thorough research was conducted to ensure a strong familiarity with the development, missions and position of this important unit. Logically the research flowed into the role of China, both a historical perspective and very contemporary issues. U.S. policy currently points toward raising the presence and commitments in the Pacific. Current documents as well as a historical review give context to the ebb and flow of U.S. involvement with Indonesia. Research of the literature sets the stage to analyze issues the U.S. faces with regard to the Kopassus.

[40]Ibid.

[41]Ibid.

After the review of pertinent research topics two additional research questions were nominated in conjunction with the primary research question. Chapter 3 explores the process used to analyze these three questions.

CHAPTER 3

RESEARCH METHODOLOGY

This thesis is a qualitative research study, as explained in Merriam's *Qualitative Research and Case Study Applications in Education.* The author is the primary researcher for both data collection and data analysis. The author's goal in this exploratory research is to discover and understand the role of the Kopassus inside the Indonesian military and government. This research will describe how the U.S. for years supported, trained with and then disengaged with the Kopassus. The author will explain the incidents of human rights violations that made this unit infamous and prevented U.S. engagement for the last 12 plus years. This will include a look at the current worldview through the lens of recent media coverage on Kopassus and annual reports on human rights abuses/allegations in Indonesia. Finally, the author will analyze the impact of U.S. non-engagement, the value of reengaging and recommend productive approaches.

Data Collection and Validity

The author sought out and discussed the topic with subject matter experts in analysis of Southeast Asia and Indonesia as well as in-country military experts who worked with the Indonesian military. The author maintained e-mail contact with members of the U.S. Embassy in Jakarta, Indonesia for the latest developments with U.S. policy regarding engagement with the Kopassus. The author also discussed and received book and article recommendations from prior and current officers found on the Command and General Staff College staff panel that had experience in the Asia-Pacific region, Southeast Asia or Indonesia specifically. This includes Foreign Area Officers who worked in Indonesia and China, and continued their focus on the Asia-Pacific region. The author reached out to analysts from the Office of the Under Secretary of Defense for Policy in Southeast Asia and the Defense Intelligence Agency's Southeast Asia division and the Indonesia desk. Most contributed with recommendations for the literature research review and reviewed ideas and theories of the author during the course of research.

As this thesis covers a contemporary topic, the articles both internet and written were kept to within the last 5-10 years to provide a relatively current pulse on the situation between Indonesia and the U.S. Interviews of subject matter experts on Indonesia, South East Asia and specifically the Kopassus could not occur during this academic year in the Command and General Staff College as budget cuts cancelled many activities throughout the year. The author maintained e-mail contact with these individuals and discussed informally the concept of the thesis, searching some specifics that could be discussed and e-mailed. Due to the positions of these individuals the titles of their offices will be cited however, specific attributable names will be left out.

Books written by subject matter experts on the Kopassus, the history of Indonesia, and U.S. SOF history with Indonesia provided much of the baseline information for Kopassus growth as well as the background history for Indonesia. Additionally reports from research services and open sourced searches through the Combined Arms Research Library at Ft. Leavenworth provided many avenues to confirm issues and contemporary authors' writings.

Throughout the course of the research and analysis these individuals, as well as other Special Operations officer at the Command and General Staff College conducted

45

peer reviews of the process, content and findings. As a U.S. Special Forces officer, the author tried to avoid any personal biases by these reviews. The author acknowledges that personal biases may occur naturally as an Active duty Special Forces officer that may lean towards certain SOF centric solutions. The concept of triangulation for case studies is to use multiple data and methods to gather information from many sources for a well-rounded approach.[42] The author attempted to triangulate by reaching out to these subject matter experts in the Department of State, Department of Defense and academia. Additionally the author collected data from different historical books, articles and policies as well as contemporary versions.

Data Analysis

This topic hinges on the reader's understanding of the importance of the Kopassus inside the Indonesian military and government. Thus, the research focus is on laying the groundwork for the influence the Kopassus have had since their inception and the country's independence. This will provide the necessary context to show the Kopassus' relevance in the Indonesian military and the roles the unit played throughout the country's history.

Next, the research focus is on some of the history of U.S.-Kopassus engagement. This will reveal to the reader the timeframes the U.S. engaged with the Kopassus, when the engagement ceased, why, and the U.S.'s priorities during the same timeframe. During this part of the research, the focus will also cover human rights violations leading to U.S. withdrawal. This part will also reveal how other countries have engaged Indonesia in the

---

[42]Sharan Merriam, *Qualitative Research and Case Study Applications in Education* (San Francisco, CA: Jossey-Bass, 1998).

absence of U.S. engagement. The purpose is to show that while the U.S. withdrawal from engagement was specifically intended to punish the Kopassus, the U.S. is selectively hypocritical on units, elements and individuals it engages with.

Finally, the research looked into the administration's Pivot to the Pacific concept in the current (2013) strategy shift. To accomplish the research into the strategy shift the author conducted a review of current (within 5 years) strategy, speeches, testimonies and plans for the U.S. with regard to the Asia-Pacific region, Southeast Asia, Indonesia and specifically engagement with the Kopassus. The purpose is to demonstrate to the reader the importance of Indonesia in the current U.S. national strategy, which highlights the need for analysis into the prioritization of engagement. This also highlights where the U.S. can benefit the most for its efforts. This will be especially important as the Department of Defense faces a resource-constrained environment, where every operation must be prioritized.

<u>Summary</u>

The theoretical framework explained in Chapter 1 links the primary research question to the subordinate research questions and formulated the course of research. This framework supports the methodology and shows the importance of Indonesia to all concerned and the Kopassus to Indonesia. The analysis of these relationships, explored in chapter 4, provides the baseline to answer these research questions.

CHAPTER 4

ANALYSIS

There is only one thing worse than fighting with allies and that is fighting without them.

— Winston Churchill, *Winston-Churchill-Leadership*

Introduction

The research conducted helped the author analyze the situation from many angles to answer the original research question. How can reengagement with the Kopassus improve U.S.-Indonesian relations? To help answer that question, the author focused efforts on specifics inside the two subordinate research questions: (1) What is the significance of Indonesia with regard to the US strategy in the Pivot to the Pacific as well as Indonesia's importance to the region and China?, and (2) What is the significance of engagement with the Kopassus for the military and government of Indonesia as well the rest of the world? By answering the subordinate questions, the analysis will show why Indonesia and the engagement with Kopassus are important issues with larger effects than just a military-to-military relationship.

Many historical and contemporary authors cover the importance of the Kopassus to the Indonesian government. The Indonesian government embraces the Kopassus and there appears to be a sense of nationalism tied to the unit. The Kopassus earned a reputation, feared by those that oppose it. This is desirable as it relates to criminals and terrorists, however innocents of the population, politicians and other government employees, especially those outspoken against the government or against the current party in power share that same fear. The balance is difficult to be sure, especially in light

48

of how relatively new a unified independent democratic Indonesia is comparatively to other Muslim nations and other democratic states like the United States. The U.S. has respected SOF, which are feared by terrorists and enemy combatants, but those in the U.S. government have no worries about physical retribution from the U.S. SOF community.

While that comparison is easy to make, the U.S. does not have the internal struggles that plague Indonesia, nor the same geographical and demographic issues. In the first 60 to 70 years in U.S. history after declaring independence, the U.S. did not have a professional military as Indonesia currently does. During the same formative years in the U.S. for example, worse human rights atrocities were committed against Native Americans, Mexicans, fellow Americans and especially African-Americans. There is no way to compare the U.S. 150 to 200 years ago to Indonesia today, nor does that example forgive abuses. It does however, provide food for thought on how quickly the international community should expect a country to operate as a transparent democracy and if thoughtful guidance and good examples are more beneficial than punishments requiring self-correcting before engagement.

If modern history has given us anything to use in regards to the successful creation of a democratic government it should be a metric of how long that government can take to truly operate coherently. Is the U.S. free from police and military human rights violations? Does our system of governance respect all human rights? The questions are rhetorical and meant to provide a thought provoking perspective to U.S. aid and whole of government approach when dealing with other countries.

In most countries around the world, including the U.S., security force individuals and units participate in actions during times of crisis or intense situations resulting in a violation of what could be considered human rights. The news is rife with global examples of individuals in protest of their government, some peaceful, some resisting arrest, some inciting violence and those countries security forces responding in kind. Generally, the security forces are portrayed as the "bad guys" and it is frightening to see civilians improperly engaged by uniformed, and usually intimidating looking law enforcement officers.

In the Western world, there have been many instances in the national news where a police officer used force disproportionate to that of the individual resisting and the police officers were not convicted of a crime. This is not to compare the human rights violations of the Indonesian military with that of U.S. local or federal police. However, it is to suggest the idea that when dealing with human rights and violations of these rights, what is black and white to one culture or society is equally grey to another. Anyone on the receiving end of security forces enforcement of laws whether through riot control, arrest or interrogation likely feels like a violation in that particular humans eyes.

Human rights are thought to be universal, however even when seeking an exact definition, there are extenuating circumstances which can be brought in to change the dynamic. While it is simple to believe that the world could agree to a set of rules designed to be universally understood by all in the regard of human rights, many countries cannot agree on the definition of torture, due process of law, the limits of freedom of expression or of detainment without prosecution. The U.S. has many accusers throughout the international community due to the media's exposure of operations during the last decade of wars in Afghanistan and Iraq. The current debates on drone warfare alone have drawn critics for all political and national sides with no signs of resolution anywhere in the future. The point is that it is easy to cast judgments from the sidelines, especially when a country has no national interest or security at stake in judging another country's actions. Once national security interests are involved justification will be brought out which can counter an otherwise valid argument for universal human rights.

Additionally, to analyze how to go about implementing and judging a country's actions, culture and history are important aspects providing perspective. The questions are simple: Does rejection of engagement and international humiliation accomplish the goal of stopping human rights abuses and provide the security force and government a pathway forward? Could "behind the scenes" discussions and training from a unified front of the whole of government give an example of acceptable behavior as well as provide ground level monitoring of units by the mentors? Has any unit or leader self-corrected because of disengagement? The author realizes these are questions requiring specific, independent, in-depth case studies to answer. The concept is provided to spark thought in regards to what would the international community like to see more; a rejected unit continuing to commit human rights abuses and expected to self-correct, or a unit partnered and monitored making gains albeit minor or incremental but still making progress.

Human rights are an important part of the U.S. strategy of exporting democracy. It is a topic that must be implemented carefully, and as a part of a whole of government approach. There may be times for international outrage, accountability and allowing the humiliation of a country's government and security forces. However, these actions should be weighed against the long-term goal of setting a regional example, correcting the action in as expeditious manner as possible and providing an avenue for continued partnership.

Analysis of Subordinate Research Question 1: What is the Significance
of Indonesia with Regard to Southeast Asia, China, and the U.S.?

Indonesia remains a valuable country to the U.S. in the Southeast Asian region as an avenue to influence ASEAN, China and as way to show positive progress between a Western power and an Islamic nation. Indonesia is quite unique as a Muslim majority, Asian, democratic, archipelago multi-ethnic, densely populated country. Limiting one's view to a single attribute without consideration of the others would be remiss and like trying to analyze a car by only studying the tires and not the engine, body, interior, etc.

As the fourth most populous country on the planet, Indonesia's economic importance is on the rise as well. Indonesia's economy continues to grow, not yet taking a large percent of the population out of poverty, but has continually increased or remained steady in its GDP growth even in spite of the Asian economic crisis. Manufacturing and exports are steadily rising; however, the population growth is currently surpassing the creation of jobs.[43]

In the energy market, Indonesia transitioned from exporting oil to using its production for internal consumption and is even a current importer of oil. However, as far as liquefied natural gas, Indonesia ranks second in the world for production.[44] Therefore, what Indonesia has to offer the world is land area, sea access and a population base capable of providing cheap labor for the global market.

_____

[43]Vaughn, *Indonesia* (2011), 25.

[44]Ibid.

52

Between the economic forums of ASEAN and the East Asia Summit Indonesia keeps itself well engaged and influential among its neighbors. Indonesia borders the southern portion of the South China Sea providing an almost geographical wall between the ASEAN members and Australia or the Indian Ocean. Through the three major straits connected to Indonesia, Malacca, Sunda and Lombok over half the world's merchant tonnage and natural gas as well as one-third of the world's oil pass annually.[45] Much of these products flow to other Asian consumers in the region especially the Koreas, Japan and China. The sea connection to the Middle East and Africa for these Asian countries literally flows directly past, and some would say through, Indonesia.

There are few countries or at least regions China has not explored and began developing due to its own increased energy and product consumption. China also pays attention to the rest of the world's increased use of energy and product consumption as well. China continues to build its relationship or influence over its southern neighbors in the Southeast Asian region. The South China Sea dispute remains in the international news as possible conflicts between China and other interested countries escalate due to misinterpretation of almost any military movement. While the dispute mostly encompasses Vietnam and the Philippines, the conflict also involves most of ASEAN, including Indonesia. China prefers to deal individually with the countries contesting territory, not against a unified ASEAN front. Conflict between all bordering countries over the exact control and responsibility for the islands and Economic Exclusion Zones

---

[45]US Energy Information Administration.

boundaries prevents this unification. China considers any U.S. involvement as an "internationalization" of a regional problem.[46]

China wants to avoid conflict with Indonesia over its claims in the South China Sea, as Indonesia is an influential member of ASEAN. Indonesia originally assisted founding the association, and still sets much of the tone for the region due to population size, growing military strength and the geographical location. China's influence comes in waves, testing the opposition between military and tourist vessels visiting the area, populating the contested islands with makeshift cities and continually engaging with the contested countries. China seeks to find commonality with the other countries to show the benefit to acquiescence while at the same time subverting any efforts to stall.

While Indonesia is regarded as a developing democracy and China still claims to be a communist country, China and Indonesia share a past friendly governmental relationship. Under President Sukarno, who promoted communism, China and Indonesia saw each other as possible allies. Sukarno saw the best option for governance to be a form of communism, and was open to the relationship with China in the late 1960s.[47] Even though Indonesia went through a violent purging of communist supporters and the parties lost power, remnants and ideals remain, especially as China grows in its influence and rivalry with the United States.

Currently, Indonesia looks to China as an alternative for purchasing foreign military equipment. In the past, the U.S. focused more on training Indonesia's forces,

---

[46]Baviera.

[47]Anthony Smith, "Indonesia's Foreign Policy under Abdurraham Wahid: Radical or Status Quo State?" *Contemporary Southeast Asia* 22, no. 3 (December 2000).

especially its officers, over providing them with U.S. equipment. With Indonesia's non-alignment policy, China provides Indonesia with a more accessible and readily available option for foreign military equipment and training. Indonesia does not prefer China to the U.S., but will keep the options open to ensure it does not rely too much on any one ally. The country learned not to become too dependent on one country, much of this lesson built on its dealings with the United States.

Because of the implementation of the Leahy Conditions in the late 1990s to mid-2000s, the U.S. denied training to the Indonesian officer leadership during that time. The U.S. therefore shunned officers of influence in today's Indonesian military when they were lower or mid grade officers. Many officers were denied training solely based on being in a specific unit, not because of accusations or human rights violations. The officers who were mid-grade leaders in the TNI at that time naturally will be the senior leaders and policy makers for Indonesia today as the U.S. pivots to the Pacific.

Leaders from any country in the world base decisions on their experience. These officers throughout the TNI and Kopassus will view the U.S. through the lens of their personal and professional experiences during their careers. Recall during the time following the U.S.S.R.'s collapse, the Ministry of Defense for Indonesia chose to work with the British over the U.S., even as the U.S. was a lone super-power. Due to the U.S. strict denial of training for Indonesian officers, through their perception of no fault of their own, the experience these current and emerging officers of influence have with the U.S may not be the point of reference the U.S. wants remembered. U.S. policy therefore literally opened the door for China to become a more prominent partner force for Indonesia or at least a more viable alternative.

The international media thoroughly cover internal issues the U.S. has with budget cuts, and the desire for drastic reductions in military spending. Allies question whether the U.S. will actually be able to completely leave the Middle East, or will it keep forces near the region and potentially even continue its engagement in Afghanistan. Combined with force reductions, budget constraints and the American public's lack of desire to entertain getting involved in any other conflicts, and one can imagine how a small country with issues in a far corner of the world would see competition with China.

China is no doubt on the rise as more and more of the world becomes economically inter-dependent. Even with its regional issues, China delicately balances the perceptions of possible conflicts while openly working towards near-peer status as a military with the United States. The People's Liberation Army participates in numerous U.N. deployments, and continues to expand China's global reach for resources. China is conducting annual engagement exercises with the Kopassus. Two such exercises titled "Sharp Knife" have already occurred in 2011 and 2012, one in Indonesia and one in mainland China.[48] Therefore it is reasonable to believe that the mid and senior grade officers in the TNI and the Chinese People's Liberation Army are engaging more frequently, likely face to face many times in both countries.

These Southeast Asian nations, even Indonesia as the largest among them, realize that the U.S. only visits the region, while China is always present. Indonesia remembers well the feeling of being abandoned by the U.S. in the 1950s as well as the 1990s and even though it does not prefer China over the U.S., it also learned the lesson not to

---

[48]Office of the Secretary of Defense, *Annual Report to Congress, Military and Security Developments Involving the People's Republic of China 2012*, May 2012, http://www.defense.gov/pubs/pdfs/2012_cmpr_final.pdf (accessed March 31, 2013).

depend solely on one super-power partner. By engaging with multiple nations in partnerships, for both military training and equipping, Indonesia is posturing to lessen the leverage any one country could have over it.

Analysis of Subordinate Research Question 2: What is the Significance of Kopassus for the Military and Government of Indonesia?

> I think it's the view of the Indonesian military that without the ability to engage and train Kopassus, the American engagement and normalisation of the military-to-military relationship would be incomplete. If you don't have the relationship with the Indonesian military normalised, you can't really participate and be the leading partner in this architecture.[49]

A country's military is generally charged with protecting the country from external threats and responsible to execute their administration's strategy. In many third world countries, a nation's military is responsible for internal civil security as well as external foreign threats. The Indonesian military is a prime example of this. Due to the geographical nature of Indonesia and the many ethnicities and tribal affiliations throughout this island nation covering such a vast area, the internal conflict can appear the same as an external conflict.

Because the TNI originally operated under Dwifungsi, the country associated the government and policing actions with the TNI and Kopassus. While the Indonesian government has since removed Dwifungsi and the TNI and thus Kopassus are now no longer a policing internal security force in the exact same way, the people still associate Indonesia's protection with its military. Exceptions apply in allowing the military to operate internally as there is still a terrorist threat, and with an archipelago island chain, external can still be internal, just from a different island. Nevertheless, the idea of the

---

[49]Behm.

military no longer being a policing force is generally working. In hostage rescue situations and high-value targeting internal to the islands, the TNI and especially the Kopassus are the front-runners to quell violence.[50]

The Kopassus have a strong influence inside both the Indonesia military as a whole and inside the government. The TNI is still the most organized and strong institution in Indonesia, producing leadership personalities is common. Many of the senior political and military leaders throughout Indonesia's history have a background with the Kopassus. For example, the current Deputy Minister of Defence, Sjafrie Sjamsoeddin is a former Kopassus member. As well as General Pramono Edhie Wibowo, Chief of the Army and Major General Lodewijk Paulus the Kodam 1 commander (A Kodam is one of 12 area commands, provincial and districts).[51] Many internal and external human rights organizations consider Sjamsoeddin to be a violator of human rights.

To show the overall influence the Kopassus has on the Indonesian society as a whole, a former Vice Presidential candidate and a current Presidential contender came from the Kopassus organization. Prabowo Subianto is considered a human rights violator, yet could be the President of the Indonesia as soon as 2014. The strategy of U.S. disengagement with the Kopassus and the encouragement for prosecution of its members could then be associated with the leader of the nation, and if the U.S. has not rectified its

---

[50]Priest, 243.

[51]Defense Attaché's Office, E-mail exchanges with members and author, November 2012 to April 2013.

stance with the unit, this is the only association with the U.S. that the new president may hold.

The Kopassus Unit 81 is the most recent addition to the organization and has not been implicated in the human rights violations of the past in East Timor. It is interesting to note the U.S. has not engaged with Unit 81 solely because it is under the organizational construct of the Kopassus.[52] The individuals in the unit and the unit were created after the widely known East Timor incidents. Some of the members now, as in any direct action SOF unit are young, in fact young enough not to have been born during the times of those incidents. Yet because of association with the unit, the U.S. denies those members training and officers who are Kopassus cannot receive visas to train in the United States.

Australia considers their relationship with the Kopassus necessary to protect Australian interests in Indonesia.[53] Australian SOF works with Unit 81, as it is one of the premier counter-terrorism units in the region. While allies' actions are not an argument or proof of what to do in the face of American values, it is a point to consider. The public in Australia generally share the same values that the American public shares. Even in the face of criticisms of the engagement, Australia values the protection of its citizens, through the engagement with Kopassus over judging their human rights. Australia does not condone the actions and by all means promotes the same level of operating correctly as the U.S. does, but it does so without completely burning the relationship with a country or its leaders.

---

[52]Ibid.

[53]Behm.

Many future senior leaders in Indonesia and even a possible future presidential candidate have history with the Kopassus and associate the U.S. rejection and disengagement as an unfair judgment by the United States. The cost of limited interaction could cause a snowball effect of Indonesia rejecting the U.S. and embracing the very tactics that caused the U.S to pull back. In other words, if a unit has been successful at its task of quelling insurgency and uprisings, but has committed errors in so doing, then the U.S. should be more involved with the unit to ensure corrections in training and execution, not less. Rejection and outside judgments without full understanding can also push a country and its military to seek alternate avenues for training and equipping.

A relationship with Indonesia provides the U.S. a new avenue for establishing a relationship with a Muslim military. The media judges the U.S., rightly or wrongly, for its interaction with the militaries of Iraq and Afghanistan. Generally, the consensus of public opinion has not been positive with respect to relations between the U.S. military and its Islamic military counter-parts. In Indonesia, the relationship could be different. As Indonesia is a completely different ethnicity and culture, the soldiers would almost have a restart with ground level engagement. Indonesia is a Muslim nation, where the U.S. would be able to build a professional, mutually beneficial relationship, rather than further U.S. misunderstandings of Muslims in the Middle East and vice versa.

A positive U.S. relationship with a professional Muslim military, focused on regional security, and bringing lessons learned from a decade of war could show the world a new look at Western-Islamic relations. The current view is rocky at best, between the abrupt shut down of the Iraq war and the rise of green-on-blue incidents in Afghanistan, a positive relationship for the U.S. with an Islamic nation is needed.

Slow, short, limited interaction will not provide the U.S. with this relationship. The U.S. relationships with partner nations in non-conflict areas are not widely known. The military partnerships in the Philippines and Colombia are two operations generally outside the scope of normal public consumption for military operations. In both those countries, the military partnerships are such that the U.S. SOF, support and conventional elements assigned, deploy to the region, live and train with their partnered element and truly build partnerships/relationships. The units involved remain together until a new U.S. SOF element is brought in to replace them. The relationships provide access to the same leaders and units for years as true relationships are built and maintained.

Compared to a quick JCET of non-lethal subjects, building a new partnership would focus an entire U.S. SOF element and bring with it true leadership focus and planning. As almost no U.S. officer or NCO would have direct experience or recent lessons learned to draw from with the Kopassus, the new relationship would start from scratch. While this is generally not an issue for U.S. SOF, and often is the case, the establishment of a new, albeit conceptually renewed relationship, would be prioritized and scrutinized. No element wants additional oversight, however the pressure which comes from starting something new, and especially from being the only one to execute a mission, brings with it a level of professionalism difficult to replicate.

Additional Thoughts—Issues in Indonesia and Kopassus

Also in this time of AQN becoming harder to track internationally, the U.S. needs to integrate U.S. SOF in any available international SOF entities, especially in a Muslim majority country that could be a breeding ground for AQN off-shoots and allow them a safe-haven.

U.S. SOF and conventional forces have engaged in man-hunting high value targets in Iraq, Afghanistan, Somalia and a select few other countries. The techniques used in these countries have been honed; however techniques that work in one country do not always work in another. The Kopassus are widely renowned as expert man-hunters in Indonesia, even with the difficulty of crossing cultures, tribes, languages, urban-jungle and island hopping. The U.S. military can learn much in the realms of operating in the unique environment that the Kopassus have mastered.

In Conboy's book on the Kopassus, he makes the point of explaining how some of the unit's founders came from a TNI unit much like a military intelligence unit. A sub-set mission for the Kopassus, specifically for Group 3 is gathering intelligence. The intelligence aspect is important for the reader to understand as it shows how the unit has a history of more than just special operations, but that it had to help the greater TNI and government conduct investigations. The Kopassus are stationed throughout the island chains, and can locate and find human targets quickly, without the use of expensive technology as U.S. SOF is dependent upon. Insight into how a unit operates fluidly, between landmasses to hunt down high value individuals could be invaluable to U.S. SOF.

As the U.S. reorients toward the Pacific theater many countries where soldiers and leaders could be operating may be similar in the problems that the Kopassus operate in. It stands to reason lessons learned by U.S. SOF could benefit not only for techniques the U.S. may need to use unilaterally, but could assist in future instruction to other countries. The author personally heard an Australian exchange officer at the Command and General Staff College state, when addressing a group of students on training with the Kopassus, "just think you're going to teach them something, they will teach you about man-hunting, they are that good, really good at finding terrorists."

The analysis throughout this chapter points to pushing the development of the relationship with the Kopassus. The Kopassus supply leaders and a sense of nationalism to the TNI and Indonesia. The U.S. rejected the Kopassus for many years, largely based on the Leahy Conditions, and then a resistance for engagement until 2013. The priority for the U.S. with the Pivot to the Pacific comes at a time where new operations will be done with higher scrutiny to ensure the value of the American peoples dollars are being spent wisely. Future engagements with foreign forces must show relevance to U.S. policy and progress regional stability, while providing positive influence to neighboring countries. Partner Engagement is a concept now accepted and promoted by the most senior leaders for the military and political policy makers. A U.S. engagement strategy, implemented correctly, combined with Indonesia's demonstrated readiness to participate will generate beneficial outcomes for years.

The conclusions and recommendation found in chapter 5 draw from this analysis. The recommendation will demonstrate how to correctly implement a strategy of Partner Engagement in Indonesia and not one that will further alienate a potential ally. It is important to take an approach that strengthens our relationship rather than checking the block of engagement with a country in a way that may negatively impact our long-term relationship with Indonesia.

CHAPTER 5

CONCLUSIONS AND RECOMMENDATIONS

Conclusions

Indonesia is a country unlike any other, not only in the region, but in the world. Its culture is Asian, Muslim, democratic, multi-ethnic, and has ties to European colonialism and military tradition. Because the country is caught between an Islamic culture and a democratic government, their national identity is still forming in today's world. The country can see a common characteristic with many different countries around the world depending on what lens it chooses to look through. Through Islamic traditions, Indonesia has religious ties to the Middle East. There are also ethnic ties to the surrounding Asian nations, much like the U.S. has ties to Europe for its original founders and similarities in peoples. However, there is the governmental aspect of Indonesia successfully transitioning to a democratically elected government giving it a unique commonality with other democratic governments. While the country is rich in history, one could argue that the current culture balancing religion, multiple ethnicities, economic development, military and government power and control, is still developing its personality.

All of these cultural aspects must be taken into account and realized when dealing with Indonesia. However, as stated in the analysis the Indonesian military is a major source of pride, nationalism and is considered the strongest government institution providing the country's best leadership. Significantly, the Kopassus still have historical connections to internal and external politics because of the short history of modern Indonesia and the leaders forged in this elite unit continue to maintain influence

64

throughout the military and government. Even so and for the reasons described, the U.S. remained disengaged from this important unit in the Indonesian government and military for more than 12 years. With this understanding and acknowledgment the reasons for the disengagement and reengagement are no longer the issue, and now is the time to initiate forward progress in the U.S. relationship with Indonesia while the opportunity is present.

Looking at the examples in the analysis of chapter 4, it becomes obvious that the Kopassus' influence and connection with the Indonesian senior leadership, both military and political, is more than just a special operations element in a nation's military. The opportunity presented by engagement with this unit outweighs almost any other type of engagement in Indonesia's military. It is also likely quite a bit less expensive than most options. The opportunity to directly impact a unit that receives national and international attention because of its counterterrorism efforts and will likely contribute to the military's and possibly the nation's future senior leadership appears to be a fantastic investment strategy for the United States. Thinking in terms of setting the U.S. up with allies throughout the globe with the least strain on resources, the investment with a small but influential unit such as the Kopassus appears to be a logical choice.

A long-term approach must be taken to plan for the future where the U.S. can now affect relations with not only a military SOF unit, but also future government leaders, neighboring countries and the emerging power of China. The example can be set in a well thought-out bi-lateral approach to partnership with the Kopassus showing the greater Muslim world the U.S. rewards forward progress. The standards for respect for human rights during military operations are fluid and mistakes will continue to be made, by all military forces the world over. The Kopassus have made progress in conducting operations and the TNI has prosecuted individuals accused of human rights violations.

Disengagement from the Kopassus, as human rights organizations suggest, leaves the Indonesian military to its own devices regarding prosecution, monitoring and regulating operations. As shown in the analysis, China has shown its interest in Indonesia, as well as its interest with partnership engagement with the Kopassus. The U.S. must now evaluate if the moral lens of China is the best avenue for the Kopassus to receive partner engagement.

Continued disengagement, or focusing solely on non-lethal short term JCETs will leave the Kopassus, the TNI and Indonesia questioning the true commitment of the United States. Small investments give small returns; this much is true in finance as it is in building human capital. The U.S. cannot build trust with short duration JCETs building limited relationships on a sporadic basis. Taking a cautious approach by only engaging senior leaders in dialogues and short, non-lethal training exercises will not build relationships or trust. The Indonesian leaders will view it as an attempt at a relationship, but not a commitment. The junior leaders will not have long-term relationships with U.S. SOF's future leaders, where each can actually learn from the other.

The U.S. SOF community rotates so quickly through its assignments and positions, and the supply of forces for building capacity will not meet demand for JCETs anytime soon. Therefore, U.S. SOF, especially the Army Special Forces whose job it is to engage and train with foreign militaries, will find no shortage of work not only in the immediate Southeast Asian region, but globally. The primary purpose for JCETs are an exchange of training, with forces where a relationship is already developed and competence and operating capability of the foreign military are known quantities. U.S. SOF typically deploys for the duration of whatever the specific training objective is, usually ranging from four to six weeks sometimes a few months. JCETs are neither permanently based nor continuous.

As the research pointed out, China is interested in building partner nation capacity as well. It is fair to assume the reasons behind this are consistent with the U.S.'s reasons, to have regional stability and gain influence with possible partner nations. Additionally, much like with the U.S., having partners who purchase your equipment and train with your forces, provides avenues for other instruments of national power or at least opens the door for those other subjects. China's intentions will only be revealed by China, however viewing them as a threat will likely help to persuade them to be just that. Viewing China as an opportunity however, provides each super-power the ability to lower defenses and possibly unify goals.

The Cold War should have taught the U.S. that a strategy of mutual destruction is not a strategy to revisit. China is growing, as pointed out in the research and obvious to anyone watching the media's current reporting. Therefore, the U.S. does not need to get into another competition with an emergent super-power for allies around the globe, and especially in the region where China lives and resides. It is therefore fair to assume that a mutual relationship with a friendly third country like Indonesia could provide a pathway for long-term positive relations and common interests between the U.S. and China.

Indonesia is a strong independent country with whom both the U.S. and China wish to have good relations. China is already engaged with Indonesia and in a small way with the Kopassus. The U.S. is doing the same, and can carefully build a relationship with not only Indonesia but with China. Through a third party, the Kopassus, where ground level SOF operators help to pave the way for reassurance that all countries are interested in the same thing, a stable region.

The same standards the U.S. wishes to impart to the TNI and Kopassus (i.e. operating with the same efficiency in providing national security but with respect to human rights), the U.S. would like to share with China as well. The U.S. learned many lessons operating in the Middle East, and U.S. SOF has been at the forefront of those lessons in many cases. To share those lessons with Indonesia, and passing the concept to China could benefit the entire region.

With regard to Indonesia being a Muslim nation, both China and the U.S. could benefit from a positive relationship with Islam. By both nations engaging and sharing training and equipment, the world would see that the two super-powers, one emerging and one refocusing, can work together for the benefit of a third country, even a Muslim one. The example could help the U.S. set global precedence for positive partner-nation capacity building throughout the Muslim world. Already U.S. SOF have a training facility for Middle Eastern SOF, bringing in another competent Islamic SOF element, partnered with the U.S. and engaged by China could help to quell resistance to international assistance in the region.

It has been well over a decade since the U.S. ceased engagement with the Kopassus. The natural attrition of a unit has turned over a number of soldiers and leaders, meaning the majority of the Kopassus units are likely full of fresh faces, many born after the East Timor incidents. Historical mistakes that need investigation and possible prosecution should focus on the specific individuals, not the current unit.

Recommendations

Full Special Forces partnership with the Kopassus provides the U.S. a pathway to influence many future leaders of the Kopassus, the Indonesian military and the political realm. Leaders on both sides will spend time together training, in either country, and maintain contact throughout their careers. Conflicts prevented are hard to prove as success, as there is no way to show that a conflict would have happened if not for engagement. Successes through U.S. SOF partnerships generally are not highlighted, as continued engagement appears as business as usual. However, it is easy to see the pockets of non-engagement through history showing where the U.S. was not engaged or needed to make partnerships quickly to quell issues.

The occasional JCET barely provides a snapshot of U.S. forces and its personnel and builds minimal relations. These types of endeavors are used when needing only minimal continued development and can act as diplomatic shows of force. The JCET is great for maintaining relationships, or building upon established training. Introducing new equipment to a unit is also a useful function of the short duration engagements. Trust, a key to a good relationship of any kind and especially needed during times of crisis, takes time to build.

A SOF partnership generally exists when two units continually work together for extended periods of time, and when units have history together. The U.S. SOF element will remain with the host nation unit only departing when replaced by the next U.S. SOF element. Permanent basing and relationships are built, where the partnered SOF unit can be directly trained and evaluated continually, handing off issues or follow-up training needs to the next unit.

U.S. Special Forces partner with key units throughout the globe, mostly foreign SOF units. Currently different elements of U.S. SOF, both Unconventional Warfare (Foreign Internal Defense Teams) as well as Direct Action Units, partner with developing Afghan SOF. This was true in Iraq as well. For over ten years, U.S. SOF worked almost exclusively in Joint Operations Areas-warzones, where the security environment was difficult, yet the goals were obvious. U.S. SOF needed to provide security through improving the host nation SOF element while additionally conduct targeting of high value individuals in terrorist or insurgent networks. The Kopassus operate in a similar type of environment, albeit not a continuous warzone, but providing security while targeting high value individuals.

The Kopassus have operations they must conduct in different environments throughout the archipelago, using multiple methods of infiltration and deployment. The U.S. SOF has operated almost exclusively in the CENTCOM region for the better part of the 21st century. U.S. SOF conduct operations globally with Foreign Internal Defense through multiple programs including JCETs, however many of those programs in other regions were dramatically reduced from their pre 9/11 days. U.S. SOF's man-hunting skills of AQN and Taliban HVT's during the wars in Iraq and Afghanistan produced a force unequal in the CENTCOM AOR, which is drastically different than PACOM. Exposure to tactics, techniques, and procedures used by a competent foreign SOF in an environment as difficult as Indonesia would prove invaluable for broadening their experience again.

The exact make up of the partnerships U.S. SOF engage in around the globe vary by need. There is no one size fits all for a partnership. In the Philippines there are hundreds of soldiers working in a Joint Special Operations Task Force, with support personnel and basing. Whereas in Colombia there is only a small headquarters element from the Theater Special Operations Command (TSOC) at the U.S. Embassy and a few Special Forces teams living and working with their partner elements. The exact disposition of troops for engagement with the Kopassus needs to be evaluated with the capability and willingness of the Embassy to support and the exact missions given for the partnership.

With the Kopassus divided into five groups, there are elements of U.S. SOF that could match up specialties with each of the groups. A leadership element such as a Special Forces Advanced Operational Base (AOB), led by a field grade officer in the rank of Major (0-4) with supporting staff could partner with the Kopassus headquarters to track and advise operations. However, the Pacific TSOC, SOCPAC, could also supply a leadership element for continued partnership and connection with the PACOM. Essentially there is any number of combinations of elements that would provide a partnership advantageous for both countries.

Prioritizing a U.S. military unit for full partnership with a foreign military unit takes commitment from the U.S. Government, the assigned Geographic Combatant Commander (GCC) and the associated TSOC. The level of commitment and unit echelonment would need to be commensurate with the intentions of the U.S. Mission for long-term effect. However in light of the Pivot to the Pacific the U.S. needs to prioritize its efforts to ensure regional stability throughout Southeast Asia. Indonesia plays an important role in Southeast Asia, with influence with many countries. The Kopassus are mentioned directly by the USPACOM commander, the Secretary of Defense and numerous regional analysts, experts and journalists, all of which shows the level of influence the Kopassus has in not only Indonesia, but also the region.

Issues for Further Research

The course of this research sparked many questions and highlighted other areas of research that were not taken. These questions had to be weighed in the capability of the author to research and answer. The questions and comments that follow have been touched on in general concept, but to actually understand and answer them would require a thesis all their own. They are listed below and are generally in the same arena as this thesis as ideas or starting points for additional research.

1. U.S. SOF supplies elements of all kinds for partnerships with a unit. From Special Forces Battalions, Companies, and Detachments making up Task Forces, to Civil Affairs, Military Information Support Teams, Marine Special Operations elements, Naval Special Warfare elements and Air Force Special Operations elements; all with Foreign Internal Defense training elements. What size element, with what capabilities would provide the right partnership for the Kopassus given a decision to engage beyond the occasional JCET?

2. The U.S. can appear to be selectively hypocritical in its use of the Leahy Conditions. The U.S. has engaged with many other nations' military forces when the national interests outweighed the moral high ground of denying military assistance to leaders or units with human rights violations. Did the worldwide media attention on the Kopassus affect the U.S. resistance for engagement, while the U.S. engaged with partners in the Middle East who were guilty of the same violations or worse?

3. The U.S. repealed the Leahy Conditions on the Kopassus in the mid-2000s, yet waited until 2013 to announce a program focused on reengagement. Was the use of Leahy Conditions a means to justify non-engagement, a diplomatic game of carrot and stick for furthering other U.S. goals? Did the U.S. only decide to engage after the Kopassus began a relationship with the Chinese People's Liberation Army SOF in 2011?

4. The Leahy Conditions prevent U.S. funding to units that have committed human rights violations. The intention of the conditions forced the Department of State to vet units in South American countries, particularly Colombia, to ensure they were clean. Senator Leahy introduced the conditions in the 1990s and the Clinton administration quickly expanded them to cover any military aid to any unit. Have the Leahy Conditions positively affected any nation's military to self-improve to the point where the U.S. could once again engage? The follow-up concept here would be to analyze if depriving a foreign military of aid because of the Leahy condition worked as intended forcing the host country to prosecute individuals and reforming the unit.

BIBLIOGRAPHY

Books

Conboy, Kenneth J. *Kopassus: Inside Indonesia's Special Forces*. Jakarta: Equinox Publications, 2003.

Cribb, Robert. "The Indonesian Marxist Tradition." In *Marxism in Asia*, edited by C. P. Mackerras and N. J. Knight, 251-272. London: Croom Helm, 1985.

Hellwig, Tineke, and Eric Tagliacozzo, eds. *The Indonesia Reader: History, Culture, Politics.* Durham, NC: Duke University Press, 2009.

Merriam, Sharan. *Qualitative Research and Case Study Applications in Education*. San Francisco, CA: Jossey-Bass, 1998.

Priest, Dana. *The Mission: Waging War and Keeping the Peace with America's Military*. New York: W.W. Norton & Company, Inc., 2003.

Rabasa, Angel. *Political Islam in Southeast Asia: Moderates, Radicals and Terrorists*. Oxford: Oxford University Press, 2003.

———. *Southeast Asia After 9/11: Regional Trends and U.S. Interests*. Santa Monica, CA: RAND Corporation, 2001. http://www.rand.org/content/dam/rand/pubs/ testimonies/2005/CT190.pdf (accessed September 23, 2012).

Rabasa, Angel, and John B. Haseman. *The Military and Democracy in Indonesia Challenges, Politics, and Power*. Santa Monica, CA: RAND Corporation, 2002. http://www.rand.org/content/dam/rand/pubs/monograph_reports/2002/ MR1599.pdf (accessed August 8, 2012).

Ricklefs, M. C. *A History of Modern Indonesia Since C. 1300*. Stanford, CA: Stanford University Press, 1993.

Vickers, Adrian. *A History of Modern Indonesia*. Cambridge, UK: Cambridge, University Press, 2005.

Articles

Australian News. "US Resumes Ties with Indonesia's Kopassus Special Forces, Despite Its Past." July 22, 2010. http://www.theaustralian.com.au/national-affairs/ opinion/friendly-china-ups-ante-in-cyber-warfare/story-e6frgd0x-1226654075003 (accessed January 5, 2013).

Baviera, Aileen S. P. "The South China Sea Territorial Disputes in ASEAN-China Relations." http://nghiencuubiendong.vn/download/doc_download/377-aileen-sp-baviera-the-south-china-sea-territorial-disputes-in-asean-china-relations (accessed April 18, 2013).

Behm, Allan. "Cooperation With Kopassus? Take Care!" *Agenda* 10, no. 1 (2003): 13-18.

Bumiller, Elisabeth, and Normitus Onishi. "U.S. Lifts Ban on Indonesian Special Forces Unit." *The New York Times*, 22 July 2010. http://www.nytimes.com/2010/07/23/world/asia/23military.html?_r=0&pagewanted=print (accessed January 5, 2013).

Comer, Charles. "Leahy in Indonesia: Damned if You Do (and Even if You Don't)." *Asian Affairs: An American Review* 37 (2010): 53-70.

East Timor Action Network. "Secretary of Defense Gates Goes to Jakarta Bearing Kopassus Gift." http://etanaction.blogspot.com/2010/07/secretary-of-gate-goes-to-jakarta.html (accessed April 20, 2013).

Human Rights Watch. "Indonesia: U.S. Resumes Military Assistance to Abusive Force." July 22, 2010. http://www.hrw.org/news/2010/07/22/indonesia-us-resumes-military-assistance-abusive-force (accessed January 5, 2013).

———. "What Did I Do Wrong? Papauans in Merauke Face Abuses by Indonesian Special Forces." June 2009. http://www.hrw.org/reports/2009/06/25/what-did-i-do-wrong (accessed September 23, 2012).

Jones, Sydney. Remarks with Ernest Bower. "Are Indonesian Terror Networks Regrouping?" *BBC News*, March 10, 2010.

Noblet, Michael. "U.S. Pacific Command Engagement with Indonesian Kopassus: Recommendations for a Phased Approach." *Small Wars Journal* (2011).

Pasandaran, Camelia, and Ismira Lutfia. "United States to Lift Ban on Kopassus." *Jakarta Globe*, 23 July 2010. http://www.thejakartaglobe.com/news/us-to-lift-ban-on-kopassus/387325 (accessed January 5, 2013).

Scarpello, Fabio. "In Lifting Kopassus Ban, U.S. Should Support Indonesian Civil Society." *World Politics Review*, 29 July 2010. http://www.worldpolitics review.com/articles/6159/in-lifting-kopassus-ban-u-s-should-support-indonesian-civil-society (accessed January 5, 2013).

Smith, Anthony. "Indonesia's Foreign Policy under Abdurraham Wahid: Radical or Status Quo State?" *Contemporary Southeast Asia* 22, no. 3 (December 2000): 498-526.

United States Army Torchbearer National Security Report. *The US Army in the Pacific: Assuring Security and Stability*. The Institute of Land Warfare, April 2013.

"U.S. Resumes Ties with Indonesia's Kopassus Special Forces, Despite its Past." *The Australian News*, July 22, 2010. http://www.theaustralian.com.au/news/world/us-resumes-ties-with-indonesias-kopassus-special-forces-despite-its-past/story-e6frg6so-1225895780352 (accessed January 5, 2013).

Vaswani, Karishma, "Are Indonesian terror networks regrouping?" *BBC News, Jakarta,* March 10, 2010. http://news.bbc.co.uk/2/hi/asia-pacific/8557561.stm (accessed January 5, 2013).

Reports

U.S. Department of State. . *Country Reports on Human Rights Practices for 2011, Indonesia*. 2011. http://www.state.gov/j/drl/rls/hrrpt/2010/eap/154385.htm (accessed September 24, 2012).

Department of State. *Mission Strategic and Resource Plan FY 2013*. U.S. Mission to Indonesia, 2013.

Office of the Secretary of Defense. *Annual Report to Congress, Military and Security Developments Involving the People's Republic of China 2012*. May 2012. http://www.defense.gov/pubs/pdfs/2012_cmpr_final.pdf (accessed March 31, 2013).

U.S. Energy Information Administration. *South China Sea Full Report*. February 7, 2013. http://www.eia.gov/countries/regions-topics.cfm?fips=SCS (accessed April 15, 2013).

Vaughn, Bruce. *Indonesia: Domestic Politics, Strategic Dynamics, and U.S. Interests*. Washington, DC: Congressional Research Service, October 27, 2010.

———. *Indonesia: Domestic Politics, Strategic Dynamics, and U.S. Interests*. Washington, DC: Congressional Research Service, January 31, 2011.

Speeches/Statements

U.S. Department of Defense. "Statement by Secretary Gates at Presidential Palace in Jakarta, Indonesia." July 22, 2010. http://www.defense.gov/transcripts/transcript.aspx?transcriptid=4662 (accessed January 27, 2013).

Statement of Admiral Samuel J. Locklear, U.S. Navy, Commander, U.S. Pacific Command, before the House Armed Services Committee. March 5, 2013. http://docs.house.gov/meetings/AS/AS00/20130305/100393/HHRG-113-AS00-Wstate-LocklearUSNA-20130305.pdf (accessed April 2, 2013).